Video Classics:

A Guide to Video Art and Documentary Tapes

Video Classics:

A Guide to Video Art and Documentary Tapes

by Deirdre Boyle

ORYX PRESS
1986

The rare Arabian Oryx is believed to have inspired the myth of the unicorn. This desert antelope became virtually extinct in the early 1960s. At that time several groups of international conservationists arranged to have 9 animals sent to the Phoenix Zoo to be the nucleus of a captive breeding herd. Today the Oryx population is over 400, and herds have been returned to reserves in Israel, Jordan, and Oman.

Copyright © 1986 by Deirdre Boyle

Published by The Oryx Press
2214 North Central at Encanto
Phoenix, Arizona 85004-1483

Published simultaneously in Canada

Printed and Bound in the United States of America

∞ The paper used in this publication meets the minimum requirements of American National Standard for Information Science—Permanence of Paper for Printed Library Materials, ANSI Z39.48, 1984.

Library of Congress Cataloging-in-Publication Data

Boyle, Deirdre.
  Video classics.

  Includes index.
  1. Video recordings—Reviews. I. Title.
PN1992.95.B6   1986   016.79145'72   83-43239
ISBN 0-89774-102-1

For the old boy,
Bill Mangan,
who taught me to be a critic

and for my parents

. . . a circulation of gifts nourishes those parts of our spirit that are not entirely personal, parts that derive from nature, the group, the race, or the gods. Furthermore, although these wider spirits are a part of us, they are not "ours"; they are endowments bestowed upon us. To feed them by giving away the increase they have brought us is to accept that our participation in them brings with it an obligation to preserve their vitality.

—Lewis Hyde, *The Gift*

Table of Contents

Preface

When I was in fifth grade, Sister Mary Anthony encouraged me to keep index cards with notes on every book I read. By then, I had already developed an appetite for reading, but I was cowed by the prospect of having to annotate *all* my library finds. Although I kept file cards on everything I read that year, spurred on by Sister's gold star system of rewards, I was too overwhelmed by the incompleteness of my efforts to continue. Browsing through the stacks in the children's room in my local library, I knew I could never keep up with everything I planned to read. But the idea was planted in my mind early on that I should be widely read and keep a personal record of the literary classics I had discovered.

When I was not reading in fifth grade I was invariably plunked down in front of a tiny black-and-white TV screen watching "The Howdy Doody Show" and later, "The Mickey Mouse Club." Growing up in the Fifties meant growing up with television. It was not surprising that when the first portable video equipment started arriving in the United States in the late Sixties, many of my generation were drawn to video's flickering black-and-white images and its unprecedented access to "personal" television.

Many gravitated to video because it seemed to offer a democratic, human-sized alternative to corporately owned broadcast TV. Hippies, avant-garde artists, student intellectuals, lost souls, budding feminists, militant blacks, flower children, and jaded journalists all had a hand in staking out this new territory of alternative television. Just as the invention of movable type in the 15th century made books portable and private, video did the same for the televised image; and just as the development of offset printing launched the alternative press movement in the Sixties, video's advent launched a guerrilla television movement in the Seventies. It was actually part of a larger alternative media tide which swept over the country during the Sixties, affecting radio, newspapers, magazines, and publishing, as well as the fine and performing arts. Video's pioneers wanted to tell their own stories, express their own viewpoints, and not be interpreted or censored by the establishment media. For them, video was an alternative to the slickly civilized, commercially corrupt, and aesthetically bankrupt world of Television. Molded by the insights of Marshall McLuhan, Buckminster Fuller, Norbert Wiener, and Teilhard de Chardin; influenced by the New Journalism forged by Tom Wolfe and Hunter Thompson; and inspired by the content of the agonizing issues of the day, video guerrillas set out to tell it like it is—not from the lofty, "objective" viewpoint of TV cameras poised to survey an event, but from within the crowd, subjective and involved.

Inspired by the "happenings" and Dadaist art experiments of the Sixties, several well-known artists were drawn to video, bringing with them their already established reputations in painting and sculpture. Their prestige gave this new medium a little more respectability than it would have had otherwise. In addition to fine artists, there were also people from the performing arts—actors, dancers, and musicians—and a motley assortment of individuals with no formal art training at all, including philosophers, writers, filmmakers, and carpenters. All were attracted to the medium because it had neither history nor hierarchy nor strictures, because one was free to try anything and everything, whether it was interviewing a street bum or exploring the infinite variety of a feedback image.

In the beginning, anyone with a Portapak was a video artist, but gradually, two camps divided: artists and documentarists. The former moved freely within the worlds of conceptual, performance, and imagist art, with work ranging from sculptural environments to lyrical, computer-processed visual poems; the latter delivered countercultural statements drawn from the social and political movements of the age or crafted Whitmanesque portraits of American byways. The reasons for the fissure between them were complex, involving the competition for funding and exhibition, a changing political and cultural climate, and a certain disdain for nonfiction work as less creative than "art." But video's early years embraced art and documentary equally and stressed innovation, alternative approaches, and a critical relationship to television.

One of the great attractions then was the simple fact that video was new, virgin territory: There were no Rembrandts and Goyas of video art to haunt young video makers, no Pauline Kaels and George Bernard Shaws of video to daunt aspiring critics. Anyone with a video camera was an artist; anyone who wrote about video could be a critic. The universe of video was small enough then that even I could venture to keep a written record of everything I saw without being overwhelmed, as in my youth.

Times have changed. Video art is now taught in many colleges and art schools, and the work of major video artists is widely recognized as coequal with the more conventional art media of painting and sculpture. In 1982, Nam June Paik's work was shown at a retrospective at the Whitney Museum of American Art in New York. Acclaimed as the "George Washington of Video," Paik was the first video artist to be so recognized by a major museum in this country. And in 1986, the Museum of Modern Art in New York will mount a retrospective of Bill Viola's work. More and more, museums and galleries are including video art in their exhibition programs. And whether the general public visits such museums or not, they daily see video art's influence on high- tech, new narrative TV commercials and music videos. On the down side, video artists rarely if ever receive any credit—whether money or praise—for their contribution to these "popular art" forms. And for aspiring young artists today, it is far more difficult to get launched in the medium: Not only is the technical sophistication and concomitant expense required to make state-of-the-art video daunting—especially in a world of shrinking funding for the arts—but that free and open atmosphere of "anything goes" that pervaded video's early years has given way to academic norms and the looming achievements of video art's own Rembrandts and Goyas.

Documentary video has suffered even more from the passage of time. As the media revolutionaries grew older, they found the world radically different from the one that once celebrated the brash goals and idealistic dreams of guerrilla television. The promise that cable TV would serve as a democratic alternative to corporately owned television was betrayed by federal deregulation and footloose franchise agreements. Public television's early support for video art and documentary slowed to a virtual halt. And funding sources that had once lavished support and enthusiasm on guerrilla video groups now preferred supporting individual artists and work that stressed art and experimentation rather than controversy and community.

When broadcast of portable video tapes became possible in 1974, the rough vitality of guerrilla TV's early days was shed for a slicker TV look. Ironically, without anyone really noticing, television absorbed guerrilla TV's innovations, transforming them into the parody of mock-u-entertainments such as "Real People" and "That's Incredible!" Although many guerrilla TV groups have long since disappeared, a number of pioneers continue to keep alive their ideals: Some, like DeeDee Halleck of Paper Tiger Television, continue to produce work for public access cable; others, like Greg Pratt—a documentary producer for a Minneapolis CBS affiliate—now work within commercial television; and a few others, like Jon Alpert—a freelance correspondent for NBC's "Today Show"—work as independent journalists. Some younger people, new to video, have begun using the consumer formats of VHS and Beta to produce works with promising echoes from the past, from eye-opening documents on the struggles in Central America to poignant interviews with a grandparent.

Video, once a term that elicited quizzical looks from the uninitiated, has become a household word. The recent home video boom has put a VCR (videocassette recorder) in nearly every home, much like that proverbial chicken in every pot. Whether it be the surveillance camera guarding the elevators in your high-rise apartment building, the latest punk video your children watch on MTV, or the movies on tape you borrow from a rental library, video has become part of the fabric of everyday life in America. Sadly lacking from its texture, though, are these independently produced works.

Because I know that video is more than just a cheap way of seeing feature films or recording TV shows and movies off the air, because I think that many people would enjoy seeing the best original video productions made during the last 15 years—if only they knew about them—I decided to annotate a basic collection of video classics, inspired no doubt by Sister Mary Anthony's assignment so many years ago.

WHAT IS A VIDEO "CLASSIC"?

I took into account a number of different factors in arriving at this list of 80 titles, which includes the work of more than 100 video producers. Although the first American video art tape was made in 1965 by Nam June Paik, the earliest tape listed here, David Cort's MAYDAY REALTIME, was made in 1970. This is more a reflection of the as yet limited preservation and distribution of early video works than of their enduring interest.

Fifteen years of video classics must, of necessity, include the work of such video art pioneers as Nam June Paik, Ed Emshwiller, Frank Gillette, William Wegman, and Peter Campus, to name only a few, as well as some of the guerrilla television made by groups like TVTV. Equally important are the younger generations of artists who have risen to international acclaim, artists such as Bill Viola, Mary Lucier, Edin Velez, Dan Reeves, and Dara Birnbaum, among others. A number of broadcasting firsts are also highlighted, such as the first independent video documentaries to be aired on public television— TVTV's LORD OF THE UNIVERSE—and on network television—the Peabody award-winning THE POLICE TAPES by Alan and Susan Raymond. Given the low-cost affordability and widespread diffusion of portable video equipment, people in such unlikely media centers as Johnson City, Tennessee, and Milwaukee, Wisconsin, could all produce tapes, and titles that represent such regional diversity are prominently featured in this collection.

By drawing attention to the art of video, this guide is intended to help pave the way to increased archival video preservation and encourage more critics, scholars, librarians, programmers, students, and young video makers to examine this rich past. Since *Video Classics* was primarily designed as a core collection for public, academic, and special libraries, media arts centers, and museums, I tried to focus on the overlapping interests of these varied institutions. Universities with departments of art, journalism, television, and media studies, music, American studies, popular culture, and women's studies will all find tapes guaranteed to be of interest to their students and faculty. Museums and galleries new to video will find candidates for their developing video archives and exhibition programs. Cable and broadcast programmers searching for new directions in information and entertainment programming may find some of their answers charted by independent producers.

It was the broad range of public libraries and their media collections that presented the greatest challenge. I found myself being influenced by my split-level life, commuting between New York City and Southbury, Connecticut, a conservative, exurban community far from the fast-paced lifestyles and avant-garde artways of New York. As a frequenter of Southbury's public library, I realized how many libraries around the country, with little or no tradition of media services but with an avid population clamoring for the latest in video "movies," were developing video collections with no idea of this parallel universe. No reputable public library collects only best-selling novels; public libraries are compelled to provide a balanced collection that ensures patron access to information and artistic expression as well as popular entertainment. Believing the same requirements for book collections should also apply to video, I thought about how a selection guide, designed mainly for larger, sophisticated media collections and their users, could also serve the interests of ordinary viewers all over the country. Whether *Video Classics* is used as a collection building tool or merely as a reference book, it will introduce viewers to the multifaceted world of independent video.

Whenever possible, I included video art that is readily accessible, even familiar, to the general public. For example, the techniques developed by Kit Fitzgerald and John Sanborn for INTERPOLATION have become part of the vocabulary of music videos and TV commercials; Jane Veeder's MONTANA raises video game imagery to the level of art; and Max Almy's DEADLINE and PERFECT LEADER are music videos with a difference: Rather than promoting a band and a song, she uses the latest computer graphics technology to analyze and comment on our late-20th-century culture.

Given the startling regional diversity of the United States (which is virtually ignored by the mass media), I selected documentaries that highlight the particularities of America as well as the talents of artists from all over the country. I was guided by my belief that we as a people still harbor intense curiosity and respect for our differences. Here you will find tapes about New Orleans's music and Minnesota's writers, Philadelphia's MOVE and Wisconsin's dairy queens, Hmong immigrants in Rhode Island and Eskimo athletes in Alaska, Chicano low riders in California and black double-dutch champs in New York. More than anything, these tapes are about people: a Vietnam vet, an Italian grandmother, a junior high school student, and a backwoods moonshiner. From giving birth to dying in a hospital or languishing a lifetime in prison, they explore the harsh realities of life while also celebrating its joys. Here you will find comedy, drama, poetry, and music, politics, labor struggles, and media analysis. Taken in sum, this collection represents a capsule history of the issues and art of the last 15 years. Not all viewers will be interested in every classic tape, but there is something here for everyone.

ACKNOWLEDGMENTS

This book owes its being to a number of individuals and organizations who were helpful to me during various stages of its writing. First and foremost, I am indebted to all the artists listed here for having created work that has been a gift in my life. Passing that gift on to others is a labor of gratitude that completes the circle. I am grateful to these artists and their distributors for providing me with preview tapes as well as detailed credit information and photographs. Many of the reviews first appeared, in different form, in the pages of *American Film, Library Journal, Sightlines, TeleVisions, Videography, VideoPlay,* and *Wilson Library Bulletin.* I am especially grateful to Robert Beck and Lisa Krueger of Electronic Arts Intermix for service above and beyond the call of duty and to Marita Sturken, author of the Museum of Modern Art's excellent video catalog, for allowing me to borrow upon her insights and research in writing these annotations.

I appreciate the interest of my colleagues and students at The New School for Social Research and Fordham University College at Lincoln Center and the many insights I've gained from my students over the last eight years. Jack Churchill persuaded me to continue this book at a difficult juncture; I can now say how glad I am for his excellent advice and encouragement. Stephen Calvert proofread the manuscript, offering not only expert editorial advice but the priceless enthusiasm of a layman first reader: I can not imagine writing a book without his help. Anne Thompson and Penny Wolfson of Oryx Press are remarkable for their patience; I am grateful to them both for their understanding and professionalism.

Although I received grants to conduct research for another book on the history of documentary video, the fruits of that research also proved invaluable in writing this book, and so I gladly acknowledge my enormous gratitude to the New York State Council on the Arts, the Port Washington Public Library, and the John Simon Guggenheim Memorial Foundation for their support and encouragement of my work. Finally, I am grateful to my parents, who gave me a quiet country home to write much of this book and who, over the years, have given unstinting emotional and financial support for my often precarious writing life.

June 1985

Introduction

Video Classics consists of 80 reviews arranged alphabetically by title. It opens with a title index to the 101 works included in this book. This disparity in numbers reflects the fact that several titles are actually collections of shorter works by a video artist. These 80 tapes were chosen from a much larger universe of original video productions; many works are not included here, not because they are inferior but because this book is designed as a manageable, beginning acquisitions tool for media librarians, archivists, and programmers. A number of tapes which I would have liked to include are no longer in distribution; perhaps increased interest in early video production will render such tapes available again. Subsequent editions of *Video Classics* can update this list and expand it to reflect not only other artists' work but additional titles by producers already in this edition. After the reviews, readers will find an Artists/Producers Index, a Subject Index, and a Distributors List.

Every review includes basic mediagraphic data: the title of each tape, the principal creative person(s) responsible for it, copyright date, length, whether in color or black-and-white, the distribution source(s), and the video formats in which it is available. All tapes are available for sale, most are available for rental, but prices have not been listed because they vary from distributor to distributor and are subject to change. Although the institutional prices for most original videotapes remain considerably higher than for consumer-oriented, feature films on tape, most distributors are willing to bargain on the prices for half-inch formats, so collectors should make a point of inquiring about lower rates. Not included here is information about availability of tapes for cable, public, or network television; many tapes exist on one-inch masters—some have also been transferred to the European standards, PAL and SECAM—but negotiation for the broadcast or cable rights for each tape should be discussed directly with the distributor.

Many reviews also include detailed credit data, listing the names of creative staff involved in the production and post-production of the tape as well as information about funding. Since there is no standardization of terminology employed in writing video credits, staff titles vary from entry to entry. Some standardization was attempted in organizing information by slightly rearranging the order devised by individual producers to make it easier for users to read. I relied entirely upon the information provided by producers and distributors, supplemented by my own notes. Regrettably, there are many gaps. I hope that artists will make a point of providing such information for future editions of this book, since the value to scholars and researchers in having detailed credit data can be considerable.

Nearly all of these tapes have won awards and/or been shown in video festivals, exhibited in museums, and broadcast on public television. I asked the producers and distributors to indicate what awards their tapes had received, and a list of such prizes is included wherever that information was provided. This is by no means exhaustive, and the absence of any listing of awards does not necessarily mean a tape is without prizes.

Although each review focuses on the individual work, some remarks on the artist's background are usually included, particularly if he or she has been a pioneer or major force in the development of the medium. Longer reviews generally signify a major work in a given genre or a tape by an important artist or documentary producer. Whenever titles appear in small caps in the text, it signifies that a review of the tape is included in the book. Titles of tapes not reviewed here are in italics. Based on nine years of writing and thinking about video and its amazing evolution, these reviews represent my own critical response to the best and/or most representative work by American video artists and documentarists. I strongly advise that readers determine the advisability of acquiring a work and showing it in public not on the basis of critical recommendation but by actually viewing and evaluating the work themselves.

The Artists/Producers Index includes, in addition to videotape makers, their artistic collaborators. For example, dramatist Sam Shepard and actor Joseph Chaikin are listed with video artist Shirley Clarke for their collaboration on TONGUES. The many staffers who worked on each production are not listed in this index: Without comprehensive credit information, such incomplete indexing seemed pointless at this time.

The Subject Index is divided into 26 categories which range from adolescence to women's issues. Subject headings were developed to suit the contents of the tapes, which are listed under as many headings as appropriate. Genre headings for art and documentary are also included here.

Finally, the Distributors List provides names, addresses, and—when listed—phone numbers for the sources of all the tapes mentioned in this book. Readers are advised to contact distributors directly for catalogs and up-to-date price lists.

Alphabetical Listing of Titles

Video Classics:

A Guide to Video Art and Documentary Tapes

Reviews

After Montgolfier

by Davidson Gigliotti

1979. 11 min. color.
Distributor: MOMA. Formats: ¾″, Beta, VHS.

Credits: *Executive Producer* Peter Bradley *Production Assistant* Craig Sinard. Produced by KTCA/TV.

Awards: Red Ribbon, American Film Festival.

AFTER MONTGOLFIER is an exhilarating first-person voyage in a hot-air balloon. Video artist Davidson Gigliotti trains his camera downward on lush midwestern farmlands, affording viewers the vicarious thrill of floating effortlessly high above the earth. But there is more to this trip. Gigliotti, rather like the Wizard of Oz, lifts us up above Minnesota—instead of Kansas—for a voyage that traverses time as well as space. Drifting above the pastoral horizon, we glimpse the world as did the pioneering French inventors and aeronauts, the Montgolfier brothers: from the perspective of the pre-industrial Romantic age. Beyond being an unpretentious, delightful slice-of-life documentary, AFTER MONTGOLFIER is also a homage to the landscapes and sensibilities of 18th-century artists and visionaries.

Davidson Gigliotti was an original member of the Videofreex, one of the first video collectives formed in the late Sixties, when half-inch video was first sold in the United States. When the Videofreex left New York City for rural Lanesville, NY, Gigliotti became interested in landscapes and was among the first video artists to translate a painterly interest in the closely observed natural world to tape.

Algebra and Other Menstrual Confusions

by Connie Coleman and Alan Powell

1984. 8 min. color.
Distributor: Coleman & Powell. Formats: ¾″, VHS, Beta.

Credits: *Narrator* Bill Wheeler *On-line Editor* Mark Focker. Produced at Experimental TV Center, Owego, NY, and Videosmith, Inc., Philadelphia, PA. *Post-production* Videosmith, Inc. *Funding* National Endowment for the Arts/American Film Institute Media Arts Fellowship, administered by Pittsburgh Film-Makers Inc. and Pennsylvania Council on the Arts.

ALGEBRA AND OTHER MENSTRUAL CONFUSIONS is a rich and witty autobiographical exploration of male-female aptitudes for mathematics, among other things. The tape opens with graphically stylized feet dancing to a lively beat, a carefree image of adolescence. Suddenly, a male voice-of-God narrator starts reciting mathematical problems: "Two ships are out to sea. If one is traveling at . . ." Surreal images— vividly colorized and computer-processed—of cars, ladders, earth-moving equipment, and swimmers illustrate these problems, which become increasingly ironic statements of veiled sexuality. Juxtaposed with these fantastical images and relentless puzzles are Coleman's memories of high school: wearing circle pins and mohair sweaters, stuffing paper in her bra and being caught smoking in the ladies' room. Her singsong voice accompanies a computer-generated notebook with penciled diagrams, mathematical equations, and snapshots of Coleman and her friends at the beach, at the prom, and at school. The marvelous irony here is how Coleman brilliantly undermines these stereotypical notions of feminine incapacity for mathematical, abstract thought with her own impressive computer mastery.

Coleman and Powell have been working together in video since the mid-Seventies. Alan Powell was a founding member of Electron Movers and an intern at the National Centre for Experiments in Television in San Francisco. Over the last ten years, the couple has produced a significant number of extraordinary image-processed tapes, including *Southern Exposures, Radiation Therapy,* and *Glass Vibes.*

Always Late

by Mitchell Kriegman

1979. 10 min. color.
Distributors: Castelli/Sonnabend, Shadow Projects Inc. Formats: ¾",
VHS.

Credits: *Producer/Director* Mitchell Kriegman *Performers* Susan Blommaert, Mitchell Kriegman *Camera* John Keeler *Lighting* John Budde *Editors* Mitchell Kriegman, Bill Marpet. Produced in association with the Television Lab at WNET/13: *Executive Producer* David Loxton *Supervising Engineer* John J. Godfrey.

Awards: Fifth Annual Ithaca Video Festival.

ALWAYS LATE offers a new twist on the Rashomon motif: the tale told from multiple, conflicting viewpoints has become the saga of a young couple with relationship problems. They are seated on a couch—are they at home or in their therapist's office?—each telling their own version of why they were late for a recent dinner party. As their anger with each other escalates, the differences in their accounts grow more and more exaggerated and hilariously absurd. Their resolution is simple: They will never leave their apartment again. Borrowing on soap opera shtick, ALWAYS LATE probes deeper into the ways couples battle with their incompatibilities.

Kriegman, a gifted comedian with a biting satiric wit, plays the young man here and in all his tapes. He began his career as a writer and became interested in producing his own wacky brand of existential video humor in the mid-Seventies. Although his work bears some resemblances to that of video artist William Wegman (see THE BEST OF WILLIAM WEGMAN), Kriegman cites his major influences as television, Latin American novelists, vaudeville—his grandfather was a Chicago orchestra leader at vaudeville's height—and his parents, a psychiatrist and psychologist who told stories about their patients' histories over the dinner table. Not surprisingly, his work focuses on vulnerability: the private uncertainties, fears, and failures that plague everyone. His tapes—audio and video—have been shown in museums, galleries, and video festivals as well as on public and network television.

Ama L'Uomo Tuo (Always Love Your Man)

by Cara De Vito

1975. 30 min. b/w & color.
Distributor: EAI. Formats: ¾", VHS, Beta.

Awards: Best of Festival, Women's Video Festival; Best Documentary, First Ithaca Video Festival.

This is an intimate portrait of the videomaker's 75-year-old Italian grandmother, who speaks about her life and Old World–style marriage. The portrait opens with Adeline Lejudas taking the subway to an Italian club; a passionate rendition of an old ballad is heard in the background. The sequence immediately establishes Adeline's rich ethnic heritage, her upbeat sense of humor, and her earthy charm. Although we see Adeline as a vital person today, shopping, cooking, and cleaning, De Vito's real focus is on their heart-to-heart conversation about her 50-year marriage, her reasons for marrying—"I used to live with my brother and my sister-in-law, who was very mean to me. . . . And one day I says, 'If there comes a horse with a head on and a pair of pants, I'm going to marry him, as long as I get out from here'"—and the unexpected horrors she endured. Adeline strays from housewifely advice into a terrifying description of male prerogatives, including violence and the power of life and death over a family. Her anguished story of a forced abortion, which nearly caused her own death, provides the tape's gripping climax. But in an extraordinary dining sequence, in which the camera is placed at a distance to observe the family interaction, we see the patterns of behavior handed down from father to son which she unwittingly perpetuates. Adeline's deeply ironic parting comment to her granddaughter— "Always love your man, no matter what"—expresses the code she has accepted and by which she has lived.

Made during a time of increasing interest in family roots and of growing feminist consciousness about the psychological and sexual abuse of women, the tape offers a complex view of one woman and, implicity, the social structure that molded her, leading viewers to further thoughts about women's traditional roles and power. The portrait is infused with affection for her gutsy grandmother, but De Vito wisely leaves ambiguous any analysis and interpretation of her life and actions.

Sensitive camera work, relatively complex sound mixing, and fine editing mark this half-inch videotape as an exceptional documentary for its time; it won kudos at major video festivals and a local public TV broadcast in New York. De Vito, who began making videotapes in 1972, later went on to produce for the independent documentary series "Changing Channels" on Minneapolis public TV and, more recently, made a film on domestic workers.

American Grizzly: Frederick Manfred

by Mike Hazard and Jim Mulligan

1983. 28 min. color.
Distributors: CIE, UCVideo. Formats: ¾", VHS, Beta.

Credits: *Directors* Mike Hazard, Jim Mulligan *Producer/Writer* Mike Hazard *Narrator* Charles Brin *Reader* Robert Bly *Camera/Editor* Jim Mulligan *Sound* John Calder, Chuck Preston, Micky Chance, Mike Rivard, Woody Smith *Music Score* Gregory Theisen *Musicians* Gary Crow, Mary Emberley, Jay Johnson, Greg T. Zeitgeist *Graphics* Cats Pajamas.

Awards: American Film Festival; Kijkhuis Festival, Netherlands.

Hardy had Wessex, and Faulkner, Yoknapatawpha County; novelist and screenwriter Frederick Manfred has his own imaginative country: Siouxland, where Iowa, Minnesota, Nebraska, and the Dakotas abut, where the Sioux Indians once lived and Manfred himself grew up. "The best discipline in the world for someone who wants to be a

writer is to have grown up in the farm country," Manfred says. "A farmer farms soil; a writer farms brain cells." Jim Mulligan's camera captures the beauty and richness of Siouxland in this lyric view of an American writer and his native land.

Nominated for the Nobel Prize in Literature, Manfred is like his fictional characters, larger than life and twice as romantic. His deep, sonorous voice—whether reading from his stories or commenting on the relationship of the Indian *wakon* to quantum mechanics—weaves a spell over his listeners, presenting a heroic, masculine view of pioneering and adventure. Poet Robert Bly concludes the tape by reading a passage from Manfred's *Lord Grizzly,* which seems to sum up the achievements of an exceptional literary man.

Mike Hazard has been experimenting with novel ways of introducing poetry and prose in his series of literary portraits, which includes Minnesota poets Meridel Le Sueur, Robert Bly (see A MAN WRITES TO A PART OF HIMSELF), and Tom McGrath. His successful efforts at sharing both the life and work of these regional—and national—treasures are well worth our attention.

Artifacts

by Woody Vasulka

1980 (©1981). 21 min. b/w & color.
Distributor: EAI. Formats: ¾″, VHS, Beta.

Woody Vasulka, in collaboration with his wife, Steina, has been in the vanguard of the electronic arts since the early Seventies. With the help of designer Jeff Schier, they pioneered the Digital Image Articulator, or Imager. Their tool converts a video picture to digital numbers that a computer can understand; once a video image is digitized, it can be stored in computer memory—the framebuffer—and manipulated in countless ways. The Imager can perform continuous zooms, multiply a frame so that the picture becomes magnified to the point where the entire frame is only one- picture-element (pixel) big, or combine several frames to produce extraordinary images of common objects.

ARTIFACTS opens with Vasulka, dressed casually in overalls, standing in front of his kitchen stove, peering into the camera and bemusedly stroking his beard. He takes his own image and manipulates it through the Imager, multiplying it into numerous postage-stamp likenesses that zoom in and out in rhythmical pulse. This gridlike mosaic is further manipulated by flattening and elongating it, accompanied by the amplified sounds produced by the video synch signal. The artifacts consist of both Woody's camera-generated image and unanticipated experimental images arrived at by the Imager. In another sequence, Woody's hand reaches out for a ball in which a feedback image—an infinite number of hands and balls—can be seen. Like an electronic crystal ball, the images within this magic circle transmute, reverse left-right polarities, and alternate from black-

and-white to color. The image of his own hand is transformed into a ghostly, surreal vision.

ARTIFACTS is a sampler of some of the exercises an artist can devise to demonstrate, in Vasulka's words, "rather simple arithmetic operations." This gloss belies the wit, humanity, intellectual play, and exhilaration Vasulka's challenging inventions present. (See also SELECTED TREECUTS by Steina.)

Vasulka came to the United States in 1965 from his native Czechoslovakia, where he had studied film and engineering. After producing several films here, he began to explore electronic sounds and images and invent new video tools. In 1971, in collaboration with Steina, he founded The Kitchen, one of the first exhibition centers in the country for experimental video. Since then, the Vasulkas have achieved exceptional acclaim for their technical innovations in the international world of video art.

Ballet Classes: A Celebration

by Jack Churchill

1985. 60 min. color.
Distributor: VFC Productions. Formats: ¾″, VHS, Beta.

Credits: *Audio/Assistance* Bill Churchill, Jean Churchill, Phred Churchill, Lynne Conroy, Alex Griswold, P.K. Smith *Piano* Martha Yacyshyn *Additional Piano* Alexandra Bacon *Still Photographs* Margaret Richardson *Calligraphy* Sharon Crowley *Teacher* Jacqueline Cronsberg *Students* Leslie Bilosz, Sara Ann Grow, Paige Tiffany Hall, Todd Hall, Susan Harris, Anne-Marie Hartley, Sarah Marxer, Ashley Anne Pope, Anita Ravi, Ashley Richardson, Gianna Russillo, Karen H. Taylor, Heidi Wolfe, and other students of Ballet Workshop, Sudbury, MA. *Thanks* Deirdre Boyle, Dorothy Etheridge, Henry Felt.

BALLET CLASSES is the first in a series of tapes that focus on the long, demanding process of training to become a dancer. Former filmmaker Jack Churchill spent eight years following the development of several talented students at Ballet Workshop in Sudbury, Massachusetts, under the direction of their exceptional teacher, Jacqueline Cronsberg. The tape takes the viewer through the various stages of a typical class and ends with an extraordinary master class, where a bevy of beautiful young ballerinas display the skill and grace their training has taught them. The viewer need not know a thing about ballet to discover en route the glorious process of learning to be one's best. And for the ballet lover or parent of a hopeful dancer, these behind-the-scenes views make the sacrifices and considerable effort needed to become a ballet dancer vivid and admirable.

More than anything, BALLET CLASSES is about the relationship between a dedicated teacher and her gifted students, and Churchill's patient camera singles out those revealing moments when expert guidance coupled with effort and the sheer joy of doing something you love illuminate the complex learning process. Jacqueline Cronsberg's voice is heard over the opening sequences of students at the barre: "It's a wonder anyone ever becomes a dancer! You're working against your own body, and nobody has perfection." Despite the known limits, she affectionately and gently encourages her students to "Hold your position," "Feel the pain of fifth," and ultimately, "Be gorgeous!" As she patiently adjusts feet, legs, arms, necks, hands, and wrists, we are reminded of the infinite number of factors each dancer must have constantly under control.

As the tape unfolds, several students emerge as major characters who will reappear throughout: graceful Suie, who recovers balance in a penché arabesque, lively Anne-Marie, who can touch her bun; the lone boy Todd, who crashes into people; and sultry Gianna, who must watch her hand. Occasionally their high spirits erupt, revealing some teasing competition, but more often their relationships are supportive, communicated by a gentle pat on the shoulder given by an older girl to a younger one whose jump has just been praised.

Churchill cuts from an in-class correction to a living room packed with girls watching the replay. Paige, who winces with frustration over her mistakes, relives the moment and discovers what she was doing wrong. Later, Ashley, the beautiful, long- legged blonde with an effervescent personality, grabs the microphone to deliver an exuberant testimonial to Mrs. Cronsberg: "She has confidence in us. She tells us we're good so we'll try harder. And she does everything like New York City!" Even as Ashley and Anne-Marie ham it up for the camera, they admit that class is the most important thing in their lives, and hint at the sacrifices their families have made for them to study.

In the closing section, Cronsberg echoes the girls' earlier comments, marveling at families who are willing to give their children a chance for a dance career and at children who must make major decisions about their lives while they're still little girls. "Mrs. C's" confidences are heard as her students warm up for class, stretching out each other's feet or lending a hand to someone pirouetting. Their grace and accomplishment then soar in a *tour de force* performance that climaxes with a lyrical slow-motion sequence of jumps. Churchill holds each girl breathlessly in midair, partnering them as they defy gravity and reach beyond themselves. "I'd rather you went for it and fumbled than to not have tried at all," Cronsberg tells them, urging them to attempt a lunge that becomes a larger metaphor for their lives as dancers.

13

Barbara Buckner: Selected Work

by Barbara Buckner

1981. 24 min. color.
Distributor: EAI. Formats: ¾″, VHS, Beta.

Credits: Includes three works: *Hearts* (1979. 12 min.), *Heads* (1980. 6 min.), and *Millenia* (1981. 6 min.). Produced in association with the Television Lab at WNET/13. *Funding* New York State Council on the Arts.

Barbara Buckner's poetic sensibilities found their best expression when she discovered electronically processed video in 1972. Finding video a more malleable medium than film, Buckner gravitated to the Experimental TV Center, where she had access to tools for analog and digital computer image processing being created by outlaw engineers like Dave Jones. Working with voltage controls, Buckner was able to adjust precisely the video signal, the color sine wave, or the frequency of audio oscillation. Becoming a master of video cybernetics, she was free to explore her own visions.

In the three tapes anthologized here, Buckner abstracts real objects into subtle articulations of light and color and feeling. *Hearts* is probably her most popular work. The plural title refers to the many meanings overlayed in this symbol: the physical heart pumping life-giving blood to the body, the heart as the emotional center of the self, and the romantic impulse. The looming image is the graphic shape of a human heart poised over a landscape. According to the various feeling states it traverses, the heart pulses rhythmically, speeding up and slowing down, and shifts color from subtle pastels to chartreuse, orange, and gray. Its landscape contains a house and two people who cryptically move inside and out. Cosmic storms seem to lash this house, turning the sky a blinding, sulfurous yellow. From out of nowhere comes a pendulum, angularly swinging to divide the elements; later, waves of light paint the horizon with soothing shades. Without a prosaic narrative, the viewer easily understands the visual poem of a throbbing heart, its metaphor for romantic love, and the more cosmic notion of a pulsating life awake to the mysteries of the universe.

Heads appears at first to be a rather whimsical work, consisting of an unlikely series of images of heads: man, woman, pig, horse, lamb, child. The pig is shown with an apple cut-out of light on its head, the horse with a horseshoe over an eye. But Buckner's modulation of these images transforms them into more complex figures. The woman's solarized head looks alternately like the profile of Nefertiti, an X ray image, and a death mask. The child's image, with a checkerboard band superimposed on its forehead, is haunting; it becomes transformed into a ghostly figure, the pale remnant of some survivor framed by orange and green towers looming menacingly behind.

Millenia consists of another series of disparate images with titles—geometry, animals, men, moons, and the dead—that seem to recapitulate the history of life on earth. Beginning with mathematically complex grid patterns, formulas for creation, Buckner moves to a Noah's Ark–like procession of camels, lions, ducks, and zebras, moving along like colorful targets in an arcade game. Men play games (is it baseball or war?) and their movements evoke Eadweard Muybridge's locomotion studies. Crescent and full moons in pink and blue reproduce in gridlike wipes across the screen, an evocation perhaps of the female role in this history lesson. Finally, lovely swirling particles of light travel in columns at the culmination of the tape. Buckner's mystical intuitions are luminously revealed in these short, playful, mathematically precise works. Her exceptional ability to strip away the mundane to reveal the profound makes her work compelling.

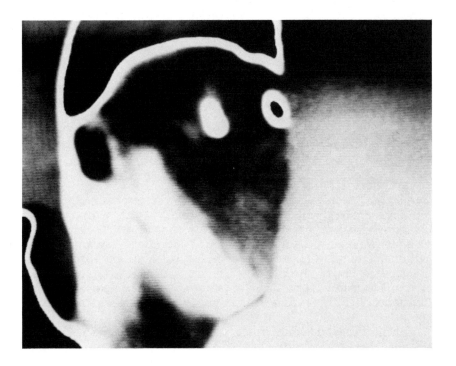

The Best of William Wegman (1970–78)

by William Wegman

1981. 20 min. b/w & color.
Distributor: EAI. Formats: ¾″, VHS, Beta.

The key to the deadpan humor in William Wegman's tapes is their simplicity. Recorded without edits or any pretense of technical sophistication, Wegman's brief improvisational sketches depend upon absurdist visual gags that create odd discontinuities between what is seen and what is said. Called by some "The Buster Keaton of Video," Wegman reminds one of pioneer video comic Ernie Kovacs, who designed inventive work for the small, flattened space of the TV screen. Wegman's tapes have appeared on "The Tonight Show" and "Saturday Night Live" as well as in museums and galleries around the country.
    Using black-and-white video and a stationary camera, Wegman stands before us, slightly disheveled and fully dressed, explaining while he sprays an entire can of deodorant under his arms how it keeps him dry all day and free from worry about social nervousness. In another sketch, he smiles broadly while explaining how he suffered from terrible fits of rage and depression until an electroshock treatment froze a smile on his face. He's still depressed, he confesses, but now everyone thinks he's happy. In yet another skit, his belly bare, he assumes two voices, speaking—as it were—through his navel.

Although Wegman frequently performs alone, using simple props such as a book or two reflector bulbs, his zaniest moments are with his weimaraner dog, Man Ray, whose mournful expression always seems to tremble on the brink of meaning. Together they are a classic comedy duo. In Wegman's best-known sketch, Man Ray sits beside him as he corrects the dog's spelling errors and explains the difference between "beach" and "beech." Man Ray looks confused, cocking his head to one side. Finally, Man Ray licks Wegman's face. "Oh, I forgive you," Wegman concedes.

The Best Place to Live

by Ralph Rugoff and Peter O'Neill

1982. 55 min. color.
Distributor: Best Place Video. Formats: ¾", VHS, Beta.

Credits: *Camera* Peter O'Neill *Sound* Ralph Rugoff *Editing* Peter O'Neill, Ralph Rugoff *Production Assistants* Kao Her, Lawrence Budner, Coco Fusco, Toua Kue *Research/Translations* Louisa Schein *Archivist* Jon Schwartz *Archival Assistant* Patricia Gorra, Chris Szabo, Mark Gentzel *Videotape Editor* Dell Setzer *Technical Consultant* Wilson Chao *Narrator for Translations* Sara Ting *Humanities Consultant* William O. Beeman *Subtitles* WGBH Caption Center. *Funding* Rhode Island Committee for Humanities, National Endowment for the Humanities, Rhode Island State Council on the Arts.

Awards: Red Ribbon, American Film Festival.

THE BEST PLACE TO LIVE is a sensitive documentary about the changing lives of members of a five-year-old Hmong community in Providence, Rhode Island. Exiled from Laos for their part in aiding the CIA during the war in Southeast Asia, the Hmong struggle to adapt to a new life without abandoning their own traditions and love for their native land. Documentarists Rugoff and O'Neill focus on five Hmong people whose experiences point up the conflicts they face here.

The tape opens with a naming ceremony for a one-month-old baby. While a rooster is killed—to summon the baby's spirit into his body—children watch a Daffy Duck cartoon on television. At a soccer match, we meet 28-year-old Pheng, who spent his youth, from age 14 to 22, fighting in the war. His blood and nerves were made in war, he says, and he feels he cannot change, despite his peaceful life in America. Pheng narrates a montage of Laotian war footage, explaining how the remote mountain Hmong, unconcerned with politics, were enlisted to fight with the Americans because of their land's strategic importance as a military zone. In his role as interpreter, Pheng introduces us to a man being interviewed by a welfare worker.

17

He is obviously broken by his wartime experiences and reports he is unable to hold a job because he is haunted by evil spirits. The scene is poignant because the welfare worker seems not to understand that the man's mind is "not in order," urging him to look for a part-time job and go to English classes.

In another scene, caught in a web of misunderstanding by community officials and residents, Hmong witnesses are questioned by exasperated city police officers after a Hmong student is stabbed by a black student outside their high school. A funeral director "suggests" that they hold their services at home when 140 families tie up business for over a week with traditional funeral rites.

Subtly revealing the complex issues facing the Hmong, O'Neill and Rugoff allow them their own voices, presenting the viewpoints of the entire Hmong community, including women, teenagers, and elderly religious and clan leaders. The documentarists' patient efforts to be accepted by them—acquiescing to limits set on what could be taped—yield a luminous, intimate document of the Hmong and their plight as strangers in a strange land.

Black, White and Married

by Philip Mallory Jones and Gunilla Mallory Jones

1979. 58 min. color.
Distributor: Philip Mallory Jones. Formats: ¾", VHS.

Credits: *Additional Camera* Henry Coshey Linhart, Lance Wisniewski *Music* Al Lambert, Cary Joseph. Produced in association with the Television Lab at WNET/l3: *Supervising Producer* Carol Brandenburg. *Post-production Assistance* TV Workshop at WXXI, Rochester, and the Experimental TV Center, Owego.

Awards: Atlanta Film and Video Festival.

There are over 421,000 interracial marriages in the United States and 54% of all Americans disapprove of them, according to BLACK, WHITE AND MARRIED, which profiles four middle-class interracial couples: black actress and model Marcia McBroom and her husband, psychologist Ira Landess; John Ford, the black mayor of Tuskegee, Alabama, and his social worker-wife Tas; two Memphis, Tennessee, lawyers, Richard Fields and Deborah Brittenum; and the videomakers themselves. Subtle, lyrical glimpses of couples making a child's bed and families eating breakfast or strolling in the park convey the nature of their daily lives. Interviews explore the couples' feelings about their partners, their children, and the social approval or disapproval of their marital choices. Several note that the hardest thing is simply being married and living with another person. The tape doesn't reveal dramatic events nor does it offer penetrating sociological or pyschological insights; instead, it persuasively presents a normal, affectionate, everyday portrait of interracial marriage.

Prompted by the lack of serious attention given interracial marriages by the mass media—the two-dimensional couple in "The Jeffersons" and the interracial courtship in *Guess Who's Coming to Dinner* hardly did justice to the situation—the Joneses produced this thoughtful tape. (Ironically, they are now divorced.) In 1971 Philip Jones cofounded the Ithaca Video Project, devoted to the development and appreciation of video as an art form. The couple was responsible for the long-running, successful traveling show, the Ithaca Video Festival, which showcased the best video art and documentary tapes annually from 1975 until 1984.

Cape May: End of the Season

by Maxi Cohen

1981. 5 min. color.
Distributor: Video Repertorie. Formats: ¾″, VHS, Beta.

Credits: *Producer/Director* Maxi Cohen *Camera/Sound* Joel Gold, Bill Marpet, Maxi Cohen *Equipment* Rebo Associates. *Funding* National Endowment for the Arts, CAPS grant.

Awards: Golden Athena, Athens International Film and Video Festival; Judge's Choice, Atlanta Film and Video Festival.

Maxi Cohen plays with her interviews in CAPE MAY: END OF THE SEASON and creates a short tape that is charming in its simplicity and whimsy. Her focus is on retired folks on vacation. They are found in postcard compositions, standing snapshot-still on the beach or, unaware of the camera, casually watching the world go by from a park bench. In answer to her questions—What did you have for breakfast? For dinner? What advice do you have?—her senior citizens respond with wit and obvious gusto. Editing a litany of favorite foods—fresh ham, veal parmigiana, string beans, and all the coffee you could drink!—Cohen assembles their answers to create amusing juxtapositions and reveal just how mellow and wise these vacationers really are. What could have been a travesty of age is, deftly handled, a lighthearted celebration.

Maxi Cohen has been making videotapes since the early Seventies and was a cofounder of the Video Access Center, the first cable-supported public access facility in New York City. She is probably best known for her feature-length documentary film *Joe and Maxi,* a searching portrait of her relationship with her father.

Changes

by Eton Churchill

1979. 29 min. color.
Distributor: Pennsylvania State University, Audiovisual Services. Formats: ¾", VHS, Beta.

Credits: *Director* Eton Churchill *Producer* The Media Group, Pennsylvania State University.

A pregnant woman provides the emotionally gripping climax in CHANGES, a half-hour series of interviews with residents of the area surrounding the Three Mile Island nuclear facility. It opens with a school-aged girl explaining the meltdown and radiation bubble. Afraid to leave her home, she stands looking out of her bedroom window and says, "I'm not going outside again; I don't want it to happen. I'd get scared." Framed by the infamous tower, a worker at the facility tells how he has become alienated from the people he works with

21

because he no longer buys the subliminal message that everything is safe there. "If a megawatt unit melted down," he says, "it would equal all the casualties in all our wars."

Another worker speaks positively about nuclear power. He, too, works at the facility, but he argues that if they left 2,000 people working on the island, it must be OK. His anger is over the evacuation: It would have been better to send away people in poor health rather than preschool children and pregnant women.

A young schoolteacher sitting in a blossoming arbor tells how she feels about discovering she was one week pregnant during the radiation leak. She weeps openly, voicing her fears and her anger for "something I had no control over that can affect the very fabric of my life."

An older woman explains why she considers her sister a fatality of the disaster: She had invested half her money in utilities stocks, and, worried about what she would do after the leak without any income, she died of a heart attack. The tape ends with a middle-aged farm couple. They have no intention of leaving, but they feel threatened: They don't know what effect the radiation may have had on the water their livestock drank. "I know we're not the same as we used to be," she says. "We've just lost the will to push on."

These aching interviews are relentless, as Churchill assembles people whose lives and shrunken hopes mirror his own vision of the disaster. Simply shot in rich color, this tape is a powerful, persuasive document on a subject of increasing importance.

Chinatown: Immigrants in America

by Downtown Community Television Center (DCTV)

1976. 60 min. color.
Distributors: DCTV, EAI. Formats: ¼″, VHS, Beta.

Credits: *Producers/Editors* Jon Alpert, Yoko Maruyama, Keiko Tsuno *Camera* Keiko Tsuno, Yoko Maruyama *Written/Narrated* Jon Alpert *Interviews/Translations* Ting Yu, Lap Wong, Jon Alpert *Researcher* William Leung *Production Consultant* Patricia Sides. Produced in association with the Television Lab at WNET/13: *Executive Producer* David Loxton *Supervising Engineer/Videotape Editor* John J. Godfrey *Associate Director* Eulogio Ortiz, Jr. *Production Manager* Barbara Greenberg *Videotape Engineers* Juan J. Barnett, Chuck Dejan, Robert Wax *Audio/Vidifont* Francis X. Hanely. *Funding* Corporation for Public Broadcasting, New York State Council on the Arts.

Awards: Special Citation, DuPont-Columbia Journalism Award; Christopher Journalism Award for Television Excellence; Indie Award, Best Independent Television Production, Association of Independent Video and Filmmakers.

This eye-opening look at life in New York City's Chinatown probes beyond the tourist's view of an exotic culture to uncover the poverty, subhuman living conditions, and rampant economic and social exploitation of modern-day immigrants. Inside Chinatown's restaurants, kitchen staffs work more than 60 hours a week for less than $100. They scrimp and save to open their own restaurants, only to have them close due to intense competition and the highest rents in the United States. Frequently exploited by their own people, garment workers labor in Chinese-owned factories for wages and in working conditions reminiscent of the late 1800s. Women of all ages earn 12 cents for a pair of pants that later retails for $12. The Chinese Consolidated Benevolent Association runs Chinatown, maintaining the status quo by controlling jobs and business while ignoring social service needs.

For most, education is the only route out of the ghetto. Hardworking parents encourage their children's educational achievements, but pressures to assimilate into American culture often lead to family clashes, and dropouts and gang membership can dash family hopes that the younger generation will escape the crushing poverty and hard work that hem them in. Illegal immigrants are haunted by fear: In a poignant interview, an elderly man—blind from years of work in smoke-filled restaurant kitchens—tells how he has been threatened with deportation after living most of his life in Chinatown. Fear of exposure keeps many from raising their voices for a better way of life.

Also touching on housing, recreation, youth, the aged, health, attitudes to the People's Republic of China, banking, and credit,

CHINATOWN offers a glaring indictment of life in a modern-day ghetto; no one who sees it will ever think of Chinatown as simply a good place for a cheap meal again.

Distilled from over 70 hours of tape shot over a year and a half, this award-winning documentary was coproduced by WNET-TV in New York City. It is a fine example of the Downtown Community Television Center's documentary style: personal, investigative, advocacy journalism, which looks to the people, not the bureaucrats, for its vision of what the problems are. Jon Alpert is the on-camera interviewer and narrator; his homey, concerned manner stands in marked contrast to the omniscient, stand-up reporters of conventional TV-documentary fare. Though criticized at the time for the nonstop, "scolding" narration and wide-ranging, thematic overview—which flouted the independent standard of nonnarrative, observational vérité style—DCTV's style of new journalism has commanded considerable television time and critical acclaim. Begun as a community-based video access center in 1972 by Keiko Tsuno and Jon Alpert, DCTV continues to make video available to its Lower East Side ethnic community while producing feature-length documentaries and news stories for television. (See also CUBA: THE PEOPLE, VIETNAM: PICKING UP THE PIECES, and HEALTHCARE: YOUR MONEY OR YOUR LIFE.)

Chott El-Djerid (A Portrait in Light and Heat)

by Bill Viola

1979. 28 min. color.
Distributors: EAI, Kitchen, MOMA. Formats: ¾", VHS, Beta.
Credits: *Production Assistant* Kira Perov. Produced by the Television Lab at WNET/13: *Supervising Producer* Carol Brandenburg *Production Coordinator* Barbara Ravis *Associate Director* Terry Benson *Supervising Engineer/Videotape Editor* John J. Godfrey *Associate Videotape Editor* Scott Doniger.
Awards: Sixth Annual Ithaca Video Festival.

CHOTT EL-DJERID is a magical exploration of electronic impressionism and djinn-like illusions. Viola plays with light and the diffractions created by extreme heat and cold in silent landscapes of the Tunisian Sahara, Saskatchewan, and central Illinois. His series of arctic and desert mirages evoke the subtle tones of Monet canvases: pristine, opalescent skies mirrored in stark, snowy landscapes; voluptuous, liquid colors—violet, apricot, rose, lemon—shimmering in pools of desert light.

Like the 19th-century impressionists, Viola explores the natural illusionism afforded by light, but he is also intrigued by the perception of abstract and concrete realities and the narrow margin dividing them. What at first appear to be pure color compositions slowly metamorphose into concrete objects, as when two undulating lavender lights are gradually revealed to be two motorcycles traveling down a desert road. A wavy black dot on the pale horizon moves slowly toward the viewer: It is Viola trudging hip-deep in snow, haloed by twin bands of light. Heat and light animate the inanimate and abstract the concrete, forming lovely, sensuous frames of pulsating, infinitely compelling, mysterious reality.

Using a telephoto lens, Viola collapses space, foreshortening and distorting scale to create this landscape of ambiguity. He structures the tape subjectively around his own visual attention, "on how long you look at an image before you feel that you've gotten from it what you can and you move on to the next one, like looking at paintings in a gallery." Viola creates an experience for the viewer so that one can arrive at the same realizations as the artist or, better, quite personal epiphanies.

Unlike artists who view technological manipulation as an end in itself, Viola uses state-of-the-art video technology as a means of pursuing an intensely personal vision. "In the visual sense, my video works are more related to music than the printed word. They are video poems, allegories in the language of subjective perception, open to diverse individual interpretation, yet each thematically expressing specific concepts that derive from everyday life experience."

Viola began his work with electronic and acoustic sound, videotape, and closed-circuit television while in college. Uninterested in guerrilla television's freewheeling documentary experiments, he looked to avant-garde, structuralist filmmakers for inspiration. He also drew upon the legacy of surrealism, which broadened conventional notions of realism to include the stuff of the unconscious. As a child of television, he recognized the potential of the medium to touch an entire society, so he devoted much of his creative energies to developing works for broadcast. Realizing there was nothing in the design or construction of video hardware that demanded the dramatic narrative format that dominates television, he set out to develop new forms "based on the way the human eye works (as in the films of Brakhage) or on how music and electronic signals behave (as in the video of Paik)." Perhaps the key to the universality of Viola's art is his images: undulating waves of heat and light in the Tunisian desert in CHOTT EL-DJERID, a match illuminating the darkness in HATSU YUME (FIRST DREAM), a magical vase that rises and flies out a window in *The Morning after the Night of Power*. As symbols, they evoke archetypal meanings deep within the hidden recesses of each viewer's mind.

A Common Man's Courage

by Jim Mulligan and John De Graaf

1977. 30 min. b/w.
Distributor: UCVideo. Formats: ¾″, VHS, Beta.

Credits: *Director* Jim Mulligan *Producer* John De Graaf *Writers* Jim Mulligan, John De Graaf *Narrator* James M. Shields *Production Assistants* Paul Burtness, Jean Marie Ziegler, Dan Riesenfeld *Still Photographer* William Kosiak, Jr. *Sponsors* Iron Range Historical Society, Minnesota Council on Humanities.

Awards: Best Local Public TV Program, Corporation for Public Broadcasting.

A COMMON MAN'S COURAGE is the story of John Toussaint Bernard, an immigrant laborer who became a U.S. senator in the Thirties. Bernard moved to Minnesota from Corsica in the early days of the century and worked as an iron miner. After being blacklisted for suggesting a union, Bernard joined the U.S. Army and fought in World War I. He returned to join the fire department and continue his activism in the Farmer-Labor Party. While the Spanish Civil War was raging, his landslide victory in a race for Congress put him in the capital, where he was the only member of Congress to vote against the Arms Embargo Act. While in Congress, Bernard was a CIO organizer and participant in the famous Flint, Michigan, strike of 1937. Considered one of the most dynamic orators in Congress and a staunch supporter of New Deal programs, he was branded a communist during his re-election race in 1938. Bernard finally saw the arms embargo lifted—nine months after he left office and too late to stop Hitler's rise to power. He then worked in Chicago as a union organizer and against the Taft-Hartley Act, continuing his outspoken and distinguished career against all odds during the Fifties. Shown in his mid-eighties, hale and feisty as ever, Bernard appears as a hero of and for the people. "I had an accent of the tongue," he says, "not of the mind and heart."

Though in no way experimental in form—with a voice-over narrator borrowed from conventional television documentaries—it is the oral history of the charismatic Bernard and his populist, progressive causes that so distinguishes this work. Selected as best local public TV program of 1977 by the Corporation for Public Broadcasting, A COMMON MAN'S COURAGE aired as part of the "Changing Channels" series, one of the first independently produced video documentaries on public television, produced by University Community Video (now UCVideo) for public television station KTCA in Minneapolis.

Cuba: The People

by Jon Alpert, Keiko Tsuno, and Yoko Maruyama

1974. 58 min. color.
Distributors: DCTV, EAI. Formats: ¾", VHS, Beta.

Credits: *Produced/Videotaped/Edited* Keiko Tsuno, Yoko Maruyama, Jon Alpert *Assistant Producer* Carlos Diaz *Interviewers* Carlos Diaz, Jon Alpert *Editors* John J. Godfrey, Juan Barnett.

In this fast-paced overview of life in Cuba since the revolution, Downtown Community Television Center (DCTV) toured the mountains, countryside, and capital of Cuba for six weeks in the spring of 1974, talking with people about life before and after the revolution. Interviews with farmers, fishermen, musicians, construction workers, factory workers, doctors, teachers, students, religious leaders, journalists, Chinese immigrants, and children are linked by Alpert's narration, full of irony, enthusiasm, and frequent surprise at what the video team discovers. DCTV points up many improvements since the revolution—universal education, new industry, enlightened care of the mentally ill, and official recognition of Cuba's African heritage—without glossing over some deficits under socialism: Food and clothing are rationed, and public housing, although technically available to all, lags far behind demand. At tape's close, the Cubans appear to be a happy people who find life better under Fidel.

CUBA: THE PEOPLE was the first half-inch, color videotape nationally aired on public television. Yoko Maruyama flew to Tokyo to buy

the first JVC half-inch color videotape system so that CUBA could be produced in color. DCTV originally took its material to the commercial networks, which rejected it in conformity with their unwritten policy of not accepting work by independent journalists. The TV Lab at WNET agreed to air it but—since DCTV was an unknown quantity in 1974—insisted on having Harrison Salisbury, a noted Soviet expert, formerly of the *New York Times,* as a buffer. The wraparound discussion between Salisbury and Alpert offers an unexpected contrast between old-style TV journalism and DCTV's direct, informal, advocacy style. Salisbury, in pin-striped suit, cross-questions Alpert, casually clad in a T-shirt and sports jacket. Salisbury is doubtful about the sunny view of Cuba he's seen, but Alpert gently and convincingly asserts that everything DCTV presented was as they found it. UPI called it "the best look at Cuba since Castro toppled the Batista regime in 1959" and the *New York Times* wrote, "[it's] a fascinating portrait of a people who, despite well-publicized deprivations and sufferings . . . are firmly, almost ebulliently, committed to a cause."

Since then, DCTV has gone on to make video and television history, crossing over from public television to network TV with unprecedented freelance journalism for "The Today Show" and "The NBC Nightly News." DCTV has continued to serve the needs of its ethnic Lower East Side community in New York while producing numerous award-winning documentaries, such as CHINATOWN: IMMIGRANTS IN AMERICA, VIETNAM: PICKING UP THE PIECES, and HEALTHCARE: YOUR MONEY OR YOUR LIFE. A 25-minute Part II of CUBA: THE PEOPLE is also available from DCTV. This includes an interview with Fidel Castro, visits to prisons, courtrooms, Havana's Chinatown, and the Marriage Palace—"a cross between St. Patrick's Cathedral and Grand Central Station at rush hour."

Dairy Queens

by Karen Lehman, Ellen Anthony, John De Graaf, and Jim Mulligan

1982. 27 min. color.
Distributor: New Front Programming Services. Formats: ¾", VHS, Beta.

Credits: *Director/Videographer/Editor* Jim Mulligan *Sound* Ellen Anthony *Writer* John De Graaf *Story Editors* Karen Lehman, Jim Mulligan *Research/Production Coordinator* Karen Lehman *Additional Sound* Mike Hazard *Post-production Editor* Kathy Souliere *Sound Mixer* R. Jeff Smith *Music* Larry Long, Claudia Schmidt, Patty Kakac. Post-produced at KTCA-TV. *Funding* CPB grant, "Matters of Life and Death."

Awards: Blue Ribbon, American Film Festival.

The populist, progressive views readily identified with Minnesota and her native sons are reflected in DAIRY QUEENS, a look at some of Minnesota's daughters engaged in fiercely defending their land and their values. Chief among these women is Alice Tripp; with her husband, she fought a utility company that announced it would run a power line across their dairy farm and the farms of their neighbors. Demonstrations against the project drew her into long-term political involvement that eventually led her to run for governor (she received 20% of the vote) and become a national figure in the American agricultural movement.

Ann Kanten helped organize a "tractorcade" to Washington, DC, to protest federal farm policies. Shy Patty Kakac became politicized when her home and family farming tradition were threatened. These three women are the heroines of this story, fighting at home and in Washington for fair policies to ensure the survival of the family farm in America's heartland.

Ellen Anthony produced *Stay with Me,* a biography of Minnesota State Representative Karen Clark, before working on this tape. She went on to work as sign-on operator for a UHF station in St. Cloud, MN. Karen Lehman coproduced *Waters for Justice,* about imprisoned American Indian Movement leader Richard Marshall. John De Graaf, an alumnus of University Community Video in Minneapolis, has produced a number of documentaries (see A COMMON MAN'S COURAGE). Like De Graaf, Jim Mulligan got his video background at University Community Video, where he helped produce "Changing Channels." He now runs his own video production business, VideoWorks, in Minneapolis.

31

Dara Birnbaum: Selected Work

by Dara Birnbaum

1978–80. 28 min. color.
Distributors: EAI, Kitchen. Formats: ¾″, VHS, Beta.

Credits: Includes five works:
Technology/Transformation Series: Wonder Woman (1978. 7 min.):
Technical Assistance Ed Slopek, Nova Scotia College of Art and
Design; Ted Estabrook, Jim Peithman, Exploring Post # 1; Devlin
Productions Inc. *Original Television Footage* CBS Inc., "Wonder
Woman" *Soundtrack* The Wonderland Disco Band, "Wonder Woman
Disco," RS International Hippopotamus Productions.
Kiss the Girls: Make Them Cry (1979. 7 min.): *"Found a Cure"*
Ashford and Simpson *"Georgy Porgy"* Toto *"Yellow Bird"* Spike and
Allan Scarth *Vocals* Dori Levine *Audio Mix* William Allan Scarth
Technical Assistance Fred McFadzen, Ed Slopek, Nova Scotia College
of Art and Design; Ted Estabrook, Exploring Post # 1; Bruce Nickson,
Madelaine Palko, Halifax Cablevision *Television Footage* "Hollywood
Squares."
*Pop Pop Video: Part One—General Hospital/Olympic Women Speed
Skating* (1980. 6 min.) *Instrumentation* Robert Raposo *Vocals* Dori
Levine, Sally Swisher *Disco* Donna Summer.
Pop Pop Video: Part Two—Kojak/Wang (1980. 4 min.): *Instrumentation* Rhys Chatham.
Remy Martin/Grand Central: Trains and Boats and Planes (1980. 4
min.) Created for Remy Martin. *Camera and Production Assistance*
John Sanborn *Videotape Editor* Dave Pentecost, Electronic Arts
Intermix *Musical Arrangement* Kelvyn Bell, Clarice Taylor *Sound
Mix* Wayne Brathwaite *Audio Mix* Bruce Tovsky. Recorded at
Brathwaite Studios, Brooklyn, NY *Post-production Mix* Merc, Video
Arts *"Trains and Boats and Planes"* Burt Bacharach *Commercial
Footage* Sergio Valente.

In each of these five tapes, video artist Dara Birnbaum presents
familiar television images from action-adventure series, game shows,
sports, soaps, and TV commercials in order to analyze the messages
behind them. Birnbaum isolates moments, such as Wonder Woman's
transformation turn or the coy smile of "Hollywood Squares" celeb-
rity contestants, and repeats them over and over, interrupting them
with irritating emphasis until the subtler meanings imbedded in these
gestures leap out at the viewer.

In *Technology/Transformation Series: Wonder Woman,* Birnbaum
contrasts the supposedly liberated image of woman in this show with
the hidden message of her role as a sexual object. Viewed repetitively,
Wonder Woman's transformation becomes nothing more than a
dizzying pivot in place, her power nothing more than sexual allure.
Juxtaposed with these pirated TV images are songs placed as com-

mentary. Sung by a black women's vocal group, the lyrics to "Wonder Woman" seem to celebrate her superior position, but they quickly turn out to be a thinly veiled reference to sex.

Birnbaum's strategy, juxtaposing music and repetitive visual motifs, anticipates many experiments with visual patterns for music videos. However, her purpose is not to sell songs or popular media images but, rather, to "de-construct" them, offering viewers another way of seeing the values and attitudes hidden within the popular media. She artfully edits each piece to music, reordering the original TV show, as in *Kiss the Girls: Make Them Cry,* where a vibrating grid of Hollywood Squares mechanistically gyrates to a disco beat. Frequently she contrasts two images, the orgasmic shoot-out in a cop show like "Kojak" with the laser explosions in a commercial for a word processor. Birnbaum's ironic, feminist analysis goes on to compare the independent, competitive, physical strivings of Olympic women speed skaters with the whining stasis of a soap opera adulteress on "General Hospital." And in her final tape, sponsored by the liquor company Remy Martin, Birnbaum constructs a complex new wave narrative that examines how woman's body is used as a vehicle of commerce—the djinni in the liquor bottle—in newspaper, magazine, and billboard ads as well as TV commercials.

Birnbaum, whose background is in painting and architecture, began working in video in 1978, launching an international career as a video artist. Critic Benjamin Buchloh, writing in *Art Forum,* noted that "Birnbaum's work has the potential to affect the language of both art and television."

Days of Swine and Roses

by Dennis Darmek

1982. 29 min. color.
Distributor: Dennis Darmek. Formats: ¾", VHS, Beta.

Credits: *Producer/Director* Dennis Darmek *Production Assistant* Patsy Tully.

What is more American than a state fair? Dennis Darmek takes us to Wisconsin's annual celebration, where grown men stroke the sides of pigs and roses glow in the dark. Darmek's camera, snuffling close to the ground, gives us a pig's-eye view of life in the auction pen, panning up to introduce us to the Wisconsin Pork Queen, who confides that she takes a lot of harassment, like being called Miss Piggy, but finds she meets a lot of interesting people—and pigs! One porcine fellow with a cap that proclaims him a Pig Pal admits: "My wife says I'm pig crazy—as bad as wine or women," adding he's had a "hard time living down the bad-mouthing of the swine industry."

Darmek interviews two women savagely ripping up gorgeous flower arrangements; they explain for the umpteenth time that fair rules require that two-hour-old blossoms be pulped for garbage because "we strive to show you only perfection and freshness." He then moves with gentle irony to a woman selling Electric Beauty Glo Roses, artificial flowers with lightbulbs in their centers, "beautiful on the TV or night table"—and obviously immune to fair rules.

A cattlewoman explains how the fair becomes her family's home away from home for ten days, and we see her children skillfully parading their animals in competition. Elsewhere, baton twirlers in miniskirts vie for the judges' approval, their earnest performances comically juxtaposed with a contest for most beautiful dog.

Lee Scott, from Abilene, Texas, stands behind his view camera, recording Wisconsin's prime cattle and their ribbons. Telling corny jokes that are as much a tradition as the state fair itself—"Is that judge judging the front end or the udder?"—he explains what it takes to show a hefty animal to best advantage and keep it from charging off in mid-snap. The Man with the Popping Eyes talks about his years working in freak shows, and a barker demonstrating the Wonder Knife explains why people buy his products year after year, returning faithfully to the state fair, where "the people are happy, the food is good, and you don't go home with a bellyache."

Darmek's captivating view of a rural American ritual seems to bring out the ham in everyone. Combining equal parts respect and amusement, DAYS OF SWINE AND ROSES portrays midwestern America as a nice place to visit—and live. Darmek, who has never belonged to a video collective because few people make video in Wisconsin, has produced a number of entertaining slice-of-life documentaries, including *Championship Guts,* about a Frisbee tournament, and *Brewer Fever,* a portrait of the Milwaukee Brewers baseball team and its fans.

Deadline

by Max Almy

1979 (©1981). 4 min. color.
Distributors: EAI, Kitchen. Formats: ¾″, VHS, Beta.

Credits: *Production Assistants* Claudine Wims, June Rando, Dan Belmour, Jeff Lawson, Jim Haygood, Anne Turely *Editors* Norm Levy, Bob Johns. *Thanks* Museum of Contemporary Art, Chicago; One Pass Video Inc., San Francisco.

A sensuous woman's open mouth is the surreal landscape in which an emblematic jogger ceaselessly runs. Her bright red lips open and close, telling him, "Come on. You can do it. Go a little farther. Keep pushing. Don't worry. You'll make it. You've got to make it." Each

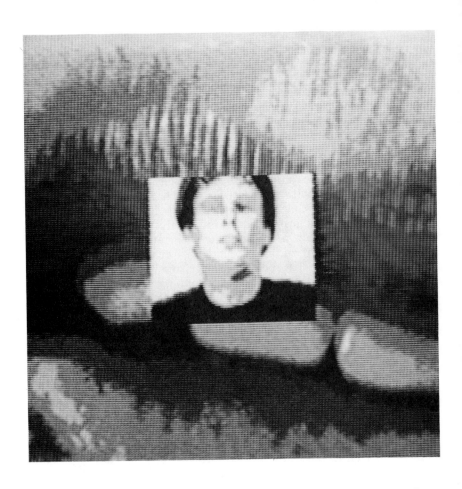

time this litany is recited, the tone shifts: The voice changes from
bland encouragement to fearful entreaty, to teasing seduction, to
menacing threat. Constantly running to stay in place, the jogger
experiences visual as well as verbal manipulation: Through sophisticated digital computer graphics effects, his image/self is squeezed,
elongated, atomized, and finally, slowed down to a nightmarish flight,
frozen in time.

DEADLINE's style should be familiar to music video fans, dazzled
by the latest in computer video graphics and special effects set to a
rhythmic beat; but what distinguishes Almy's work from the pseudo-
art of much music video is her penetrating vision. She creates an
allegory of contemporary life, imaginatively exploring the sexual politics, physical fitness, ambition, and greed of the Yuppie culture. It's a
chilling vision, but a revealing one. (See also PERFECT LEADER.)

Disarmament Video Survey

by Disarmament Video Survey Committee

1982. 30 min. color.
Distributor: Skip Blumberg. Formats: ¾″, VHS, Beta.

Credits: *Project Director* Skip Blumberg *Committee* Skip Blumberg, Wendy Clarke, DeeDee Halleck, Karen Ranucci, Sandy Tolan *Producers* 60 producers worldwide.

On June 12, 1982, a rally in support of the United Nations Conference on Disarmament was held in New York City. As a part of that demonstration 300 independent video producers collaborated to record over 3,000 interviews with people around the world—at a taxi stand in Chicago, in the bush of São Paulo, Brazil, at a school in Japan, in the English countryside, and in front of the White House—speaking their mind on the issue of disarmament. Donating time, equipment, and tape, amateur and professional producers generated 30 hours of interviews, all using the same guidelines and production format: Approach people randomly in public places and ask them to state their name, occupation, and residence and then say anything they want about disarmament within a minute. Each interview had a standard wide-angle, head- and-shoulder shot of the interviewee. No internal editing of any statement was allowed.

From the 30 hours of tape, eight hour-long tapes of the most interesting interviews were compiled. They were then shown on cable TV, as well as at community, media, and disarmament centers around New York City prior to the rally. Media vans were also set up in Times Square and the Port Authority Bus Terminal, where passersby could see the tapes and make their own taped statements; over 1,200 people recorded their views. Ultimately, an hour sampler culled from all the interviews was compiled for distribution after the rally.

DISARMAMENT VIDEO SURVEY presents an extraordinary range of individuals, who state in their own words their divergent views on disarmament. Billy Knox, from Denver, would like to limit ownership of atomic weapons solely to the United States. Carlo Povanetsi of San Francisco leaves it up to the "big man," because Carlo doesn't know much about it. Marjorie Plome from Oregon is all for nuclear development, because "when it comes down to it, there is nothing to be concerned about whether our country goes or it doesn't, because we know where our eternal home is." Selmimeron Tolla of Brooklyn is frightened for the world, for the survival of our planet. Frank Lang, who worked with nuclear weapons in the U.S. Air Force, is also frightened because he has seen how they are handled and the policies that go with them. Men, women, and children speak directly, candidly, and compellingly about their thoughts and feelings about disarmament.

Taped when this was the world's most discussed public policy issue, DISARMAMENT VIDEO SURVEY reveals video at its grassroots best, turning a frequently passive medium into an active one, a forum for an exchange of ideas and debate. Putting a human face on statistics generated about our attitudes toward disarmament, the survey goes beyond confirming them to provide the human presence—the furrowed brows, the reflective pauses, the personal touches of real people expressing their views—lacking in signatures on petitions and percentages in opinion polls.

The SURVEY emerges from a tradition of political video making begun in the late Sixties during the era of antiwar activism and mass demonstrations for social and civil rights. It suggests that the best impulses of guerrilla television to decentralize the television medium—so that it functions as a communication medium of and by the people—are still alive today.

Ends of the Earth: Plaquemines Parish, LA

by Andrew Kolker and Louis Alvarez

1982. 70 min. color.
Distributor: Center for New American Media. Format: ¾".

Credits: *Producers/Directors/Writers* Andrew Kolker, Louis Alvarez *Camera* Andrew Kolker *Sound/Narration* Louis Alvarez *Editor* Terry Skiner *Music* The Balfa Brothers, Alma Bartholemy. *Thanks* Eddie Kurtz, New Orleans Video Access Center, Bay Area Video Coalition, Chronicle Productions. *Funding* National Endowment for the Arts, Alabama Arts Council.

Awards: Blue Ribbon, American Film Festival; Atlanta Film Festival; Silver Dubloon, Mardi Gras Film and Video Festival; AFI National Video Festival.

The era of political dynasties dies hard in Louisiana, as demonstrated in Louis Alvarez and Andrew Kolker's fine portrait of the powerful, corrupt, two-generation political family that ruled Plaquemines Parish with an iron fist. Judge Leander Perez, a notorious bigot and shrewd businessman who parlayed his political power for multimillion dollar interests in the oil-rich marshlands of his parish, was a charming, colorful, amoral figure who might have stepped out of a Tennessee Williams play. Like the tragic king in a Greek drama, he succeeded in passing on his power to his sons but sowed the seeds of ruin that would lead to their demise in a desperate struggle for ultimate control. Kolker and Alvarez follow this inevitable denouement, having assembled an impressive array of historical documents—archival films, old television broadcasts, newspaper clippings—and eyewitness reports by politicians, lawyers, old-time parish residents, and journalists who help them trace the fascinating rise and fall of the Perez dynasty and the end of a political era.

Kolker and Alvarez were members of the New Orleans Video Access Center (NOVAC), a major video production center operating on behalf of the city's low-income, black population during the Seventies. Among other projects, they produced "Being Poor in New Orleans," an independent documentary series for local network television that won numerous prizes for journalistic excellence. As partners in the Center for New American Media, they have since made a number of award-winning documentary tapes about the lifestyles and languages of regional America. (See also THIS CAT CAN PLAY ANYTHING.)

Four More Years

by Top Value Television (TVTV)

1972. 60 min. b/w.
Distributor: EAI. Formats: ¾", VHS, Beta.

Credits: Wendy Appel, Skip Blumberg, Nancy Cain, Steve Christiansen, Mike Couzens, Bart Friedman, Chuck Kennedy, Chip Lord, Anda Korsts, Hudson Marquez, Martha Miller, T. L. Morry, Maureen Orth, Alan Rucker, Ira Schneider, Michael Shamberg, Jody Sibert, Tom Weinberg, Megan Williams. Additional material courtesy of Marc N. Weiss, Barbara Kopple, Laurence Storch and Vietnam Veterans Against the War. *Thanks* Carol Bernstein, W. H. Ferry, Audrey Sabel, The Vanguard Foundation, Cypress Communications Inc., Sterling Manhattan Cable Television, Teleprompter Inc., Video Tape Network, CTL Electronics, Technisphere Inc., The Egg Store.

One of the first documentaries to be shot entirely on portable video equipment, FOUR MORE YEARS made history with its you-are-there view of the 30th Republican National Convention. Instead of pointing their cameras at the podium, TVTV's crew of 19 threaded its way through delegate caucuses, Young Republican rallies, cocktail parties, antiwar demonstrations, and the frenzy of the convention floor. Capturing the hysteria of political zealots, they focused on the sharp differences between the Young Voters for Nixon and the Vietnam Vets Against the War, all the while entertaining us with the foibles of politicians, press, and camp followers alike.

Memorable vignettes include Henry Kissinger with a look-alike child, dressed in a three-piece suit; wide-angle pans of ethnic Nixon supporters; and candid interviews with Tricia, Julie, and David, who dismiss the vets as a "small minority" while asserting that daddy is the youth candidate. One Nixon organizer's remark to her staff— "The balloons alone will give us the fun we need"—epitomizes the zany, real-life comedy TVTV captured on tape.

Interviewed on the quality of their convention coverage are press personalities whose off-the-cuff remarks ("I'm not a big fan of advocacy reporting"—Dan Rather; "What's news? Things that happen"—Herb Kaplow; "Introspection isn't good for a journalist"— Walter Cronkite) culminate in Roger Mudd's playing "mum's the word" to Skip Blumberg's futile questions.

Punctuating the carnival atmosphere are venomous verbal attacks on the antiwar vets by delegates and onlookers, who charge them with being hopheads, draft dodgers, and unpatriotic—a chilling reminder of the hostility and tragic confrontations of the Vietnam War era.

TVTV follows the chaos of the convention, editing the simultaneous events into a dramatic shape that climaxes when delegates and demonstrators alike are gassed by the police. Leavened with humor, irony, and iconoclasm, FOUR MORE YEARS is a unique document of the Nixon years. In it, TVTV demonstrated journalistic freshness and a sure feel for the clichés of this distinctive American ritual.

TVTV began as an ad hoc group formed to cover both conventions for cable television. Their success—getting both *The World's Largest TV Studio* and FOUR MORE YEARS not only on cable but on some public television stations—launched them as the hottest video group in the country in the early Seventies. They succeeded in producing two hour-long tapes on the conventions for roughly $30,000, beating the networks at their own game and, as one pundit quipped, "for the money CBS spends on coffee." At the time, the networks were using hard-wired videotape equipment, which was hardly portable. TVTV's nonthreatening presence with low-tech, portable, half-inch video equipment gave them entry to people and places that the big, burly network cameramen, burdened with heavy equipment, wouldn't think of trying. The networks viewed TVTV's pioneering use of portable video as research and development for ENG (electronic news gathering), which they would introduce shortly thereafter. ENG's "live" news style was closely modeled on the brash new look TVTV invented.

The idea for TVTV belonged to Michael Shamberg, a former *Time* correspondent and cofounder of the video think tank Raindance Foundation. In 1971, he wrote the underground manifesto of the movement and coined the term by which they would be known: *Guerrilla Television.* TVTV was a logical outgrowth of Raindance's theories about decentralizing broadcast TV, a goal made possible by the introduction of low-cost portable video equipment in the late Sixties. After the convention tapes, TVTV went on to make THE LORD OF THE UNIVERSE for PBS, landing a contract to produce several documentaries for the network, including *Gerald Ford's America, In Hiding: An Interview with Abbie Hoffman, The Good Times Are Killing Us, Superbowl,* and *TVTV Looks at the Oscars.*

TVTV's style was loosely modeled on new journalism, focused on "real people" and dedicated to making fact as vivid and entertaining as fiction. Borrowing largely from the talents of a number of filmmakers, TVTV pioneered the new video technology, moving from black-and-white to color equipment and inventing TV graphics that would become their trademark, along with their controversial use of the wide-angle lens.

Gradually, they moved from documentary into fiction, producing "Supervisions" for public TV and then *The TVTV Show,* a pilot for NBC. Talented as independent documentary makers, their skills didn't translate well or quickly enough to succeed in the competitive world of TV comedy, and the group folded after six years of historic work.

The Four Seasons

by Eva Maier

1983. 14 min. color.
Distributor: EAI. Formats: ¾″, VHS, Beta.

Credits: *Director/Choreographer/Performer* Eva Maier *Producer* Maxi Cohen. *Winter: Camera* Bill Marpet *Music* Winter from "The Four Seasons" by Antonio Vivaldi *Location Assistant* Kate Parker. *Thanks* Nancy Richards, Lyndhurst National Trust for Historic Preservation. *Spring: Camera* Bill Marpet *Music* "Springtime" by Paul Pratt. *Thanks* Budd Cook, The Nature Conservancy, Philadelphia, PA. *Summer: Camera* Robert Hertzler *Music* "Saint Bernard Waltz" (folk tune). *Thanks* Phil Pizzi, Group W Cable, Channel 2, Wildwood, NJ. *Autumn: Camera* Dena Crane *Music* "Adagio in G Minor" by Tomaso Albinoni *Set* Kikuo Saito. *Funding* Global Village Facilities Grant.

Eva Maier's post-modern dance is designed for video and unconventional settings. Over the years, Maier has demonstrated a sure feel for video space and camera optics. In her award-winning tape, *Blue Squawk,* for example, she frolicked with the contrast between foreground and background in an interplay between herself and an unlikely chorus of pecking chickens, not swans. THE FOUR SEASONS, with its four separate acts, represents Maier's most ambitious video choreography. In it she employs interior and exterior settings, a variety of musical scores, and a broader range of dance influences to explore the seasons of life as well as nature.

In "Winter," Maier is a black-clad figure whose semaphore-like gestures are etched against a white door. The camera gradually pulls out, revealing the setting to be a large glass hothouse, very formal and Victorian. Maier's shadow character executes and repeats with mathematical precision ritualized movement phrases that ambiguously suggest both the balancing of light and dark at the winter solstice and classical ballet's codified language, rendered touchingly absurd as Maier heroically struggles to realign her balance while poised on one leg, seemingly nailed to the spot. "Spring" brings the exuberance and studied innocence of the Broadway stage and musicals like *Oklahoma!*. Maier, dressed in black shorts, white shirt, and a straw hat, is seated on a bench in a pasture where several cows are grazing. She swings her legs, looking from side to side, nervously afraid to let the perky rhythm propel her along the bench. Hesitating, she gives in to the music, repeating her energetic, if seated, movements. Playing off demure innocence with girlish ebullience, her performance is about abandon and restraint.

"Summer" has her in a flowered dress, sitting in a chair on a sand dune. She rises, balances on one foot while casually kicking sand with the other foot and trailing sand from her hand. As if from a

43

transistor radio come the upbeat sounds of an ethnic waltz. "Summer" is the least complex of Maier's four seasons, with the least ambiguity and tension, as befits an idle day at the beach. By comparison, "Autumn" is weighted down not with indolence but with darkly hinted meanings. To the somber strains of Albinoni's "Adagio in G Minor," Maier stands in a high-ceilinged, formal room where everything is either painted white or covered in white sheets. Dressed in a black vest over a dark flowered skirt, Maier embodies the dark heroines of 19th-century romantic ballet; her slow, studied, elegiac movements vividly evoke the "dying swan." Moving fluidly, slowly, gracefully, her choreography is ballet-inspired yet distinctly within a modern idiom. Constantly looking over her shoulder, Maier is like a character in an Edward Gorey drawing, always aware of the macabre or absurd element that lurks in all posing.

Frank: A Vietnam Veteran

by Fred Simon and Vince Canzoneri

1981. 52 min. b/w.
Distributor: Fred Simon Productions. Formats: ¾″, VHS, Beta.

Credits: *Director* Fred Simon *Producers* Fred Simon, Vince Canzoneri, and WGBH *Engineering/Camera/Sound* Mark P. Abbate *Production Assistants* Eileen MacLennon, Susan Walsh *Post-production Assistant* Susi Dickerman *Post-production Consultant* Wilson Chao *Design Consultant* Chris Pullman.

Awards: Blue Ribbon, American Film Festival.

Frank is Frank Barber, one of 700,000 Vietnam veterans suffering post-traumatic stress syndrome after their war experiences. Hearing him tell the story of his life before, during, and, especially, after his year of combat is to accompany a man on a journey through hell. Frank is a brilliant storyteller, capable of capturing the immediacy of his past through vivid anecdotes and painful insights. Because of his thoughtful, fiercely honest disclosures, we are held enthralled by a brutal but human story that makes *Apocalypse Now* seem like a Disney fantasy. It is a relentlessly compelling account of what it is like to love killing, only to live long enough to regret it.

The tape follows Frank's story in chronological sequence. It is briefly punctuated by graphics, which fill in background information and date sequences, and by snapshots, which document his progression from a fresh-faced kid eager to win battles to a hardened soldier and, finally, to the middle-aged, puffy-faced man in rimless glasses who soberly recounts his life story.

Frank Barber enlisted in the navy in 1962 at the age of 18 and was an enthusiastic fighter by the time he arrived in Vietnam in 1969. On one fateful patrol Frank discovered four Americans brutally massacred. After that he, too, mutilated bodies and stripped them for possessions. By the time he returned home he had won the navy's Commendation Medal and a couple of Purple Hearts. When he arrived in San Diego, he expected to find a band playing, but there was nothing, nobody. His life during the Seventies became a nightmare of drugs, hostility, and sexual confusion. When he started spanking his kids, pushing his wife around, and drinking heavily, he realized he was going over the edge and went for psychiatric treatment and alcoholism counseling. Now a social worker, he still has nightmares about the war. "My feeling is that we need people to talk like I'm talking now. To be honest about what happened over there so that these guys who are walking the streets and holding this stuff inside can feel the freedom to talk about it somewhere—and not be judged for it."

Frank tells his tormented tale with an amazing degree of candor. He is soft-spoken, articulate, and dangerously controlled. He is so good a storyteller that veterans groups charged that none of his story was true, only to be disproved by his official military record. When the tape was aired around Veteran's Day, 1981, the national offices of the Veterans of Foreign Wars and the American Legion publicly objected to the tape, finding it negative and a disservice to veterans who have made successful adjustments. (A Veterans Administration study found that "about one-quarter of the roughly 2.8 million Americans who served in Vietnam—regardless of combat exposure—exhibit clinical levels of stress.") However, producer Simon is quite clear about the limitations of this tape: It is about one veteran and his experiences in Vietnam and what his life has been like since his return more than ten years ago.

Quite apart from its content, what makes Frank's soul-searching so compelling is Simon's extraordinary sensitivity and subtle direction. WGBH's Vince Canzoneri met Frank and they discussed the possibility of doing a tape. Canzoneri called Simon and the three of them developed the idea, but the style of the tape is all Simon.

Simon's video style, which concentrates on one person talking, would be, in the hands of a lesser artist, a banal "talking head," but for Simon, it is an art form born of necessity. Simon is hard of hearing and wants to see someone speaking—watch the lips move, see the messages in the eyes and facial expressions. The drama of Frank's experience and his struggle to come to terms with it and himself are all there, etched in the lines in his face, the far-off look in his eyes, his sad, ironic smiles of acknowledged self-deception.

After working in documentary video since the early Seventies, Fred Simon here achieves a *tour de force* with this portrait of an individual who is, in his humanity and frailty, a painful symbol for many others. Simon's latest work, *Men and Women: After the Revolution,* was broadcast on public television in 1985.

Giving Birth: Four Portraits

by Julie Gustafson and John Reilly

1976. 60 min. color.
Distributors: EAI, Global Village. Formats: ¾″, VHS, Beta.

Credits: *Assistant Director/Assistant Editor* Gilbert Berat *Assistants* Karen Mooney, Linda Rubin, Susan Landrey, Robert Sirignano, Anita Karl. Produced by Global Village in association with the Television Lab at WNET/13: *Supervising Engineer/Videotape Editor* John J. Godfrey *Associate Director* Henry Neimark *Production Manager* Barbara Greenberg *Production Assistant* Ruth Bonomo *Production Secretary* Stephanie Wein *Coordinating Producer* Carol Brandenburg *Executive Producer* David Loxton. *Thanks* The parents and their children, Doris Haire, Dr. David Kliot, Theresa and Angie Corrao, Col. Evelyn Skinner and The Salvation Army's Booth Maternity Center, New York Infirmary, Columbia-Presbyterian Hospital, Ken Marsh, Woodstock Community Video, The Mother's Center, Ruth Lubic, Maternity Center Association, Helene Browne, Laura Berat, Edna Reilly, Monica & Joe Rogers, Ann Butler. *Funding* New York State Council on the Arts.

Awards: Best Documentary, Athens Film Festival; Bronze Award, Information Film Producers of America.

Giving birth is a different experience for every family and every child, and this tape offers a direct, head-on look at the range of experiences and delivery options available. All the parents here were trained in Lamaze childbirth techniques, but each couple's experience varies. The first birth is in a high-tech urban hospital where an epidural anesthetic is given and a forceps delivery results. In the second portrait, a fourth child is born at home using the Leboyer method. Inserted is an interview with Dr. Frederic Leboyer, author of *Birth without Violence,* explaining that birth is a natural process, not a surgical one. Shot with a low-light camera in black-and-white, the sequence conveys a warm, quiet, and relaxed environment, in sharp contrast with the preceding brightly lit hospital delivery room. The parents of the third baby planned for a natural birth, but after eight hours of hospital labor without progress, a caesarean section is performed (off-screen). Although the father is ecstatic, the mother appears forlorn; she will be deprived of her baby until several days later. The final portrait is a celebration of birth at an innovative maternity unit where a midwife-assisted Lamaze birth is seen. Elizabeth Bing, pioneer of Prepared Childbirth in the United States, discusses natural childbirth at the tape's end.

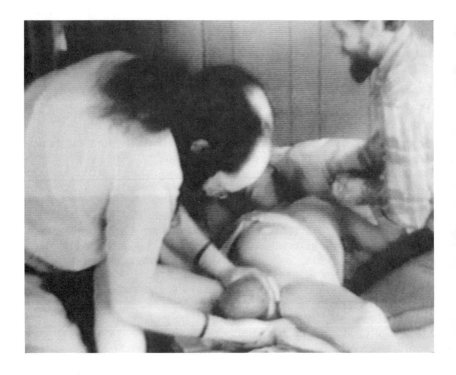

Gustafson and Reilly, a husband-and-wife video team, decided to make this tape after the birth of their son, Lars. Their hospital experience had been an upsetting one, and it led them to research what other options might have been available. Not surprisingly, their attitudes toward emergency-oriented hospital practices, which they say often ignore the mother and routinely include medication that can be dangerous to the infant, are much in evidence in the tape. But they never minimize the need for adequate medical care, especially when a real emergency arises. And the evidence that they present—healthy babies and happy parents—in the home and maternity unit sequences underscore why such deliveries are popular today.

The producers considered doing a white paper report, but they finally opted for the more intimate and informative portraits, which give graphic views of four different births that are far more informative than many training films and tapes made for expectant parents. It is obvious that a personal relationship has been formed with each couple, and this intimacy is communicated in the tape. One mother, left otherwise alone in the labor room, is gently coached in her breathing by Gustafson.

The tape, produced for public TV, begins with a teaser sequence—snippets of the four births—a television-style opener that has become a trademark in their subsequent work. John Reilly was a cofounder of New York's Global Village, a video production and resource center that has come to be identified with independent documentary production for public television. Julie Gustafson, who met Reilly as a student at Global Village, brings a deft eye, keen sensitivity, and a social conscience to her work. (See also THE IRISH TAPES and THE PURSUIT OF HAPPINESS.)

Global Groove

by Nam June Paik

1973. 30 min. color.
Distributors: EAI, MOMA. Formats: ¾″, VHS, Beta.

Credits: *Cast:* Pamela Sousa, Kenneth Urmston, Allen Ginsberg, Peggy Anne Lombard, Susan Kay Bottoms, Charlotte Moorman, Alan Schulman, Jud Yalkut, Sun-Ock Lee (Korean), Cecelia Sandoval (Navajo), John Cage *Narration* Russell Connor *Excerpts from:* "Ginsberg/Audrich" by Nam June Paik, Paul Challacombe; "Tribute to Anonymous Beauty," "Helicopter and Skating Films," "Meta- Media," and "Paradise Now" (with The Living Theatre) by Jud Yalkut; "Kontakte" by Karlheinz Stockhausen; "First Fight" by Bob Breer; "Tribute to John Cage" by Nam June Paik, WGBH-Boston; "Paik-Moorman Experiment" by Jackie Cassen, WNET/13; "The Medium Is the Medium" by WGBH Boston; "Nigeria, 1971" by Percival Borde, Binghamton Experimental Television Center. Produced in association with the Television Lab at WNET/13: *Producer* David Loxton *Director* Merrily Mossman *Production Manager* Darlene Mastro *Lighting Director* Carl Vitelli *Stage Manager* Terry Benson *Production Assistant* Diane English *Engineering Personnel* Lou Bruno, Victor Caravella, Bob Carucci, Al De Paul, Walter Edel, William Kockler, Dino Mastrojohn, Knut Olberg, Frank Pollizotto, Jesse Spain. *Thanks* Performing Arts Foundation, John D. Rockefeller III Fund, Paik-Abe Synthesizer, Rutt/Etra Synthesizer, Binghamton Experimental Television Center, Ltd., Robert Diamond.

Nam June Paik is video's preeminent artist. He was born in Korea and trained as a classical musician, going on to study electronic music with Karlheinz Stockhausen in Germany during the Fifties. Profoundly influenced by the theories of avant-garde composer John

Cage and media visionary Marshall McLuhan, Paik began to explore music's visual potential in electronic image making. Paik joined Fluxus, an idiosyncratic art group rooted more in the Twenties' Dada movement than in Sixties' "happenings." Fluxus encouraged him to take risks and combat—literally—audience passivity in his music-sculpture-performance works. By incorporating the Dadaist esthetic strategies of humor and chance, Paik succeeded in entertaining even as he shocked his audiences.

Even before coming to New York and buying the first consumer video equipment in 1965, Paik had been electronically manipulating old TV sets, rearranging their circuitry and altering their images with electromagnets in order to create anarchistic statements about art and communication. As interest in the artistic potential of television grew, he was invited along with several other artists to come to WGBH-TV in Boston to experiment in a broadcast television studio. In the first video art broadcast—*The Medium Is the Medium* (1969)—Paik's *Electronic Opera No. 1* demonstrated his unpredictable humor and subtle grasp of the medium, startling and delighting viewers and WGBH staff alike. With it, Paik turned television audience expectations upside down. He called his collage of live and taped images "low-fidelity TV," boasting he could produce images no one would

50

recognize and inviting the home audience to participate by turning off their TV sets.

A clip from this historic tape is included in Paik's 1973 classic, GLOBAL GROOVE, which he designed as a pilot program for an avant-garde laser TV station. Produced in association with the Television Lab at WNET/13 in New York, Paik worked with engineer John Godfrey, using his newly invented Paik-Abe synthesizer to colorize and electronically manipulate images. This state-of-the-art achievement would set the standard for broadcast video art for years to come.

GLOBAL GROOVE is a psychedelic collage of off-air images mixed with excerpts of Paik's tapes and films and tapes by friends Jud Yalkut and Robert Breer. No doubt influenced by McLuhan's concept of a Global Village, it expresses Paik's idealistic vision that technology could knit together a diverse world. Paik combines East and West to create a vision of multicultural television featuring performances by Korean and Nigerian dancers as well as American tap dancers. Since sponsors are inevitable, Japanese Pepsi commercials pop up between clips of Charlotte Moorman—Paik's frequent collaborator—playing the "TV Cello," John Cage relating an anecdote, Allen Ginsberg chanting "om" in sensuous synthesized color, and Richard Nixon's face "wobbulated" electronically to comic effect.

Paik's obsession with sex and music is played out as the romantic passion of Beethoven gives way to the driving rock 'n' roll rhythms of Mitch Ryder and the Detroit Wheels' "Devil with a Blue Dress On," danced to by a go-go dancer. Although some are offended by his depiction of women as sex objects—whether as anonymous dancers or as the bare-breasted Moorman wearing a "TV Bra"—another reading asserts that Paik's intention is to demolish sexist roles and taboos.

Paik's images and sounds jump dexterously about, cut with the frantic energy of a TV commercial, producing a tape that is entertaining television even as it subverts TV conventions. Since then, Paik has continued to produce his controversial, droll, often sublime video works for broadcast television—employing transcontinental satellites and lasers, the latest in communications technology—as well as producing sculptural installations for museums and galleries around the globe. In 1982, the Whitney Museum of American Art exhibited a retrospective of Paik's work, the first given an American video artist by a major museum and a significant gesture that video art had finally arrived as a contemporary art form.

51

Gotta Make This Journey: Sweet Honey in the Rock

by Michelle Parkerson

1983. 58 min. color.
Distributors: Black Filmmaker Foundation, MOMA. Formats: ¾″,
VHS.

Credits: *Producer* Michelle Parkerson *Director* Joseph Camp *Editor*
Fran Ely *Camera* WETA-TV ENG *Executive Producer* Joyce Camp-
bell, WETA-TV *Research Coordinator* Amy Horowitz *Production Photographer* Sharon Farmer.

Awards: Blue Ribbon, American Film Festival.

GOTTA MAKE THIS JOURNEY is an inspiring concert portrait of Sweet
Honey in the Rock, a radical black women's singing group. Produced
for PBS for its Independent Minority Producers Laboratory, the tape
centers on Sweet Honey's ninth anniversary concert at Gallaudet
College. Parkerson uses a deceptively simple narrative structure that
masks a formal elegance as she interweaves cameo portraits of Sweet
Honey's current performers—Bernice Reagon, Ysaye Barnwell, Evelyn
Harris, Yasmeen Williams, and Aisha Kahlil—with concert numbers
that highlight each singer and her role in the group. Rhythmically
punctuating the tape are statements by novelist Alice Walker, black
activist Angela Davis, the Reverend Ben Chavis, and feminist folk
singer Holly Near that put Sweet Honey's contribution to social
justice and American musical history into sharp focus.

It is hard to believe at first that Sweet Honey's wonderful,
soul-stirring music is all sung a cappella. The group's musical styles
range from spirituals and blues to calypso and African chants; their
lyrics are equally varied, celebrating the joys of being a woman while
lamenting political oppression and racial discrimination wherever it
exists. Anger, pride, and an earthy humor are evident in songs—
interpreted for hearing-impaired audience members—that express
solidarity with the South African martyr Stephen Biko as well as any
woman pining for a "Seven-Day Kiss."

Sweet Honey is a collective of distinctive individuals, and
Parkerson presents them each as extraordinarily beautiful and strong
women. At the hub is Bernice Reagon, a founder of Sweet Honey and
one of the original Freedom Singers, who inspired civil rights march-
ers during the Sixties. She closes both the tape and the concert with
an electrifying, Bible-thumping rendition of "Down by the Riverside,"
leading the audience into the parting lyrics "Ain't gonna study war no
more," stirring tears and a sweet sense of hope.

Michelle Parkerson, a black film and video producer, worked on
Sweet Honey's second album in 1978 and got the idea of doing a
documentary about the group. Prior to this, she produced the films

Sojourn and . . . *But Then, She's Betty Carter.* She is one of a growing number of black independent filmmakers moving into video.

Grenada: Portrait of a Revolution

by Joanne Kelly

1983. 28 min. color.
Distributor: Video Free America. Formats: ¾″, VHS, Beta.

Credits: *Camera* Skip Sweeney.

Long before the United States invaded Grenada, Joanne Kelly, a dancer and independent video artist living in San Francisco, sensed that this tiny Caribbean island was a potential hot spot. Unable to persuade likely funders of the importance of a documentary about this pivotal state—the only English-speaking socialist country in the world at that time—Kelly used an inheritance to pay for tapes and transportation for herself and her husband to visit the island.

Her tape opens with a history of the New Jewel movement, which overthrew Prime Minister Eric Gairy's government; the story is told through intimate interviews with people on the street and representatives of Maurice Bishop's government. Using vivid graphics and music to render a complex situation entertaining and clear, Kelly organized the tape thematically into units exploring social progress, woman's place, the economy, tourism, and elections, among others.

In examining the concrete factors that led to the revolt, Kelly presents some of the compelling economic concerns behind this revolution: a per capita income of $420 and a disastrous balance of trade, which meant that the country was dependent on nations like the United States for its very subsistence. Socialist Grenada's quest for economic self-sufficiency of necessity changed its economic relationship to the United States, which was not as willing as Cuba to provide Grenada with labor and equipment to reorient its economy.

Kelly doesn't gloss over some of the inherent conflicts within a revolutionary society, indicating that torture of detainees under socialist rule may have been as ignominious a practice as in previous times. However, the overwhelming message—presented by bystanders as well as officials and tourists—suggests that this new government was an expression of the people's determination to become self-sufficient. Warnings directed at United States interventionist policies are frank and, in light of subsequent events, disturbing.

When we invaded Grenada in 1983, public television stations in San Francisco, Chicago, and Los Angeles aired GRENADA: PORTRAIT OF A REVOLUTION, and network news programs, including "The MacNeil-Lehrer Report," "CBS Evening News with Dan Rather," and "Independent Network News," all featured excerpts from the tape. A nomination for an Emmy Award for best documentary provided a final tribute to Kelly's journalistic balance and intelligent assessment of trouble brewing long before the "professionals" caught on.

Joanne Kelly codirects Video Free America, a major center for video production and exhibition in San Francisco, with her husband, Skip Sweeney (see MY FATHER SOLD STUDEBAKERS). She has produced several documentaries and numerous video dance tapes.

Hamper McBee: Raw Mash

by Blaine Dunlop and Sol Korine

1978. 30 min. color.
Distributor: Korine-Dunlop. Formats: ¾", VHS.

Hamper McBee is one of the last of the Tennessee moonshiners and balladeers. "That's what slaps ya in the creek," Hamper chortles as he chugalugs some home brew while demonstrating the dying art of making whiskey—and foiling the revenuers. In a sweet and throaty voice, he sings and tells tales, revealing the lost soul trapped beneath the waxed mustache, reddened face, and traditional male role he has inherited from his daddy and other men before him. The tape is visually stunning, with exciting oblique angles that capture the light in the woods as well as Hamper's intense concentration on lining up a branch or plugging up the still. Steam hisses, wood cracks, and the fire crackles in a sensual evocation of a backwoods bacchanal that

ends explosively, courtesy of some dynamite furnished by the IRS for a humorous finale to more than just an amusing slice of regional life.

Blaine Dunlop began his career in film, then moved to video and a stint working with Broadside TV in Kentucky. He later teamed up with Sol Korine to produce this tape and *Uncle Dave Macon,* a nostalgic look at a legendary banjo player, radio hero, and leading figure in American country music. The duo also produced the

"Southbound" series for public television, focusing on southern regional life and culture and featuring Hamper McBee as its host.

Happenstance

by Gary Hill

1983. 6 min. b/w.
Distributors: EAI, Kitchen. Formats: ¾", VHS, Beta.
Credits: *Funding* National Endowment for the Arts.

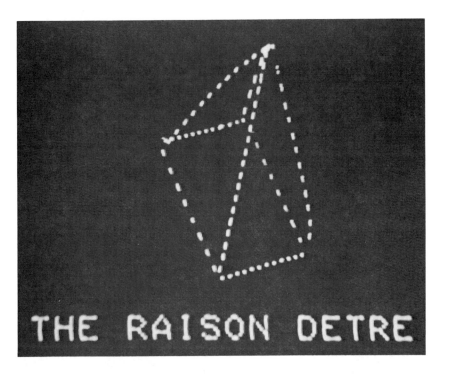

Happenstance is a circumstance due to chance. HAPPENSTANCE, Gary Hill's elegant analog computer tape, plays with unforeseen interrelationships between images and text. Trained as a sculptor, Hill started working in video in 1973, moving from exploration of synthesized video imagery to an abiding fascination with the relationships of words and objects. In HAPPENSTANCE, silvery, high-resolution images combine with Hill's hypnotic, singsong voice, creating an alternative universe of mathematical elegance and Zen-like ambiguity. Hill's words become concrete poetry, transformed into the elements of his images. He makes a tree grow out of a pile of letters, and these letters then float like leaves off a branch or fly away like birds. These word/shapes coexist with diagrammatic geometric forms—squares, circles, triangles—that frequently undulate as waveforms, curiously alive. "This is not going to be a song and dance. That's entertainment— another thing all together," he tells us, adding, "The words are going. Listen to them. Nothing surrounds them. They are open. They speak of nothing but themselves." Constructed of words that are spoken, written, and symbolically expressed, HAPPENSTANCE is finally about silence and the unexpected discovery that prompts silence. Elusive, ambiguous, and beguiling, HAPPENSTANCE is one of Hill's most intriguing narrative puzzles.

Hatsu Yume (First Dream)

by Bill Viola

1981. 56 min. color.
Distributors: EAI, Kitchen. Formats: ¾", VHS, Beta.

Credits: *Production Assistant/Photographer* Kira Perov *Thanks* Toshio Miamoto, Fujiko Nakaya, Akira Takahashi, Nobuo Nakanishi, Kyoshi Inoue, Hitoshi Ozaki, Yasuo Shinohara, Naozane Miyamoto, Keiko Murata, Koki Shibusawa, and Hokokuji Temple, Kamakura. *Man in Tokyo Night Section* Shinnosuke Misawa. *Funding/Support* Sony Corporation of Japan; United States Friendship Commission; International House of Japan, Program Office; Agency of Cultural Affairs of Japan. Produced and edited at Atsugi Plant, Sony Corporation. Produced in association with the Television Lab at WNET/13: *Supervising Producer* Carol Brandenburg.

Hatsu Yume is the first dream of the New Year in Japan, a prophecy, a new beginning. In Bill Viola's extraordinary tape, it is a model of life and death and time. Produced while Viola was living in Japan as artist-in-residence at Sony Corporation, HATSU YUME is deeply influenced by traditional Japanese culture, with its formal language of natural symbols, and by state-of-the- art video technology. Viola charts the cycle of a day that begins with light and ends with light illuminating the darkness, a cycle that metaphorically embodies the flow of time and creation. Central images of light and dark, water and mountain, life and death, fish and man are among the paired opposites entwined in Viola's all-embracing vision. His images flow associatively, as dream images do, from a forest primeval and rice fields at dawn to men fishing in the dead of night. Movement becomes imagery itself, smearing figures and colors, producing afterimages that linger beyond the fleeting light of the moment. Video treats light like water, and on the primal screen, images of death and rebirth recur, as dead fish in the market come alive in the dark sea waters.

58

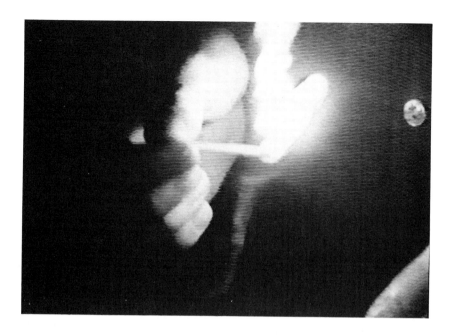

Classical images of time (the mountain and the rock) are vivid elements of Viola's personal iconography. He uses these images not because of an interest in landscape art in a European sense but as the raw material of the psyche. He explores their relationship to ideas and the deepest part of the brain: the mind. Without belonging to the Japanese culture, we still recognize the meanings imbedded in these images. Like the mountain, the rock symbolizes time, eternity, stillness. Viola first presents it speeded up to 16 times normal speed, then gradually slows to real time and, finally, down to slow motion. Looking at the rock becomes a way to see and think about time, perception, and the ineffable.

Modest as a mountain in the earth, video artist Bill Viola carries out his work without boasting of his achievements, which are prodigious in the world of international video. One of the leading innovators and technical masters of the medium, Viola has produced numerous single-channel tapes for broadcast and exhibition in museums and galleries around the world. Knowledgeable about perceptual psychology, computer mapping of data space, and principles of electronics, as well as art history, Viola has also studied Eastern and Western religious traditions and philosophies, and these rich and varied sources are evident in his art.

He began his career working with electronic and acoustic sound, videotape, and closed-circuit television in 1970. His work embraces formal, intellectually preconceived works, such as *The Red Tape* and *Four Songs,* along with more intuitive tapes like HATSU YUME. Viola always tries to begin with an image, often a poem he has written; he then realizes it by exploring the technical possibilities of the medium, pushing the limits of technology and his own artistic vision. (See also CHOTT EL- DJERID.)

Healthcare: Your Money or Your Life

by Keiko Tsuno and Jon Alpert

1977. 58 min. color.
Distributors: DCTV, EAI, MOMA. Formats: ¾″, VHS, Beta.

Credits: *Director/Narrator* Jon Alpert *Camera/Editors* Jon Alpert, Keiko Tsuno *Assistant Producers* Karen Ranucci, Victor Sanchez. Produced for Downtown Community Television Center in association with the Television Lab at WNET/13.

This devastating analysis of the disparity in health care for the rich and the poor was shot at two New York City hospitals: Kings County Hospital and, right across the street, Downstate Medical Center. The tape opens with proclamations by U.S. presidents from Eisenhower to Carter telling us that health care is a right in this country. By the tape's end, viewers will seriously question whether it is a right or privilege.

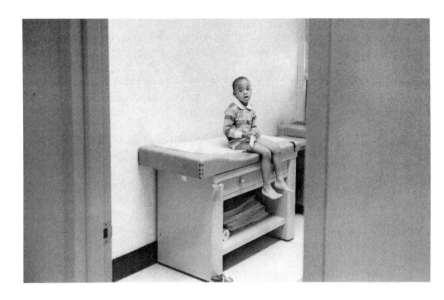

Vérité-style footage is matched with a tightly woven narration by DCTV's Jon Alpert, explaining background information on both hospitals while pointing up most major health issues in this country. The contrast between the two hospitals is glaring. Kings County's emergency room is said to be the busiest in the world. Cutbacks in staff, supplies, drugs, and vital medical equipment lead to hours of waiting, needless pain, and frequent loss of life. The wait for a clinic appointment is five months, the pharmacy is always out of stock, and the antique radiation machine for cancer treatment is called "The Killer" because it destroys so much healthy tissue. In the tape's most shocking sequence, we meet Mr. Spinelli, a heart attack patient, who is barely rescued from death one day. But days later we watch him dying on camera as his doctors, unable to find connectors for a life-sustaining machine, fumble to insert a pacemaker that won't work. The staff is competent and obviously dedicated, but they are cruelly handicapped by a system that "makes human life a commodity." "I don't see any difference between the slaughter by the Nazis and the contemptuous neglect of the authorities here," one doctor angrily tells Alpert.

Over at Downstate, a public hospital run as though it were private, patients enter only on the recommendation of a doctor. Two patients fuss over food and privacy in a sparkling research environment more like the set for a TV drama than the depressingly overcrowded corridors of its neighbor hospital. The patients seem not to suspect that matters of life and death, not comfort, are the issues besieging patients a building away. DCTV explores the underlying political issues that perpetuate such inequity, pointing up the irony of cutting aid to preventive medicine programs in order to keep overcrowded hospitals open. Moving beyond the hospitals to a Medicaid office and a pharmaceutical convention, they reveal the drug and health insurance industries that loom menacingly behind the scenes of these institutions. Alpert and Tsuno press their case, not through interviews with bureaucrats but by seeking out the stories and opinions of the people most affected by such health care: the poor, the sick, and the frightened, as well as the beleaguered hospital personnel who try against dramatic odds to serve them. By presenting a mosaic of tragic stories of ordinary human beings—a woman with MS forced to stay in the hospital far from her children because her insurance won't cover home care, a mother with a sick baby with no medicine to ease his suffering because the drugs are too expensive for the hospital to stock, an elderly diabetic with a heart condition who is afraid to check into the hospital because it would wipe out her life savings—DCTV offers otherwise mute and hopeless people a voice to protest against their health care options—or lack of them. Praised by the *New York Times* as a "devastating commentary on the state of health in urban America . . . a piercing study of hospitals and the business of medicine," the tape was broadcast as a PBS special in November 1977. It was followed by an hour-long national forum on health care, both hours provoking national discussion of a highly complex and urgent topic and some temporary improvements at Kings County Hospital.

Alpert and Tsuno had worked at New York's Gouverneur Hospital, making health care tapes, when they learned that New York's public TV station was interested in producing a series called "WNET Reports," with a segment on hospitals. Since none of the staff producers was interested in making the segment, the station contacted DCTV, and they worked for over a year researching, shooting, and editing HEALTHCARE. They were assisted by a member of Kings County's PR staff who believed in what they were doing. As a result, she lost her job. Since Alpert and Tsuno depend on city hospitals for their own health care, the tape had a personal meaning made more painful as they got to know the people whose lives and futures they portrayed on tape. (See also CHINATOWN: IMMIGRANTS IN AMERICA, CUBA: THE PEOPLE, and VIETNAM: PICKING UP THE PIECES.)

In the Midst of Plenty

by Greg Pratt and Jim Gambone

1979. 58 min. color.
Distributor: UCVideo. Formats: ¾", VHS, Beta.

Credits: *Producers/Writers/Directors* Greg Pratt and Jim Gambone for University Community Video *Associate Producer* Cynthia Fuller *Camera* Greg Pratt *Narration* Allen Hamilton *Story Editors* Mark Frost, Jim Russell *Post-production Director* Jim Mulligan *Production Assistants* John Velie, Harold Sanders, Sherry Virsen *Technical Support* Arby Schuman, Kathy Seltzer *Graphics Design* Louise Engler. Postproduced at KTCA-TV, University Media Resources, KUOM-AM. *Acknowledgments* National Rural Center, Rural America, KSTP-TV Eyewitness News, The Rockin' Hollywoods, The Horseshoe Bar, Tri-County CAP, Governor's Office of Economic Opportunity, St. James Catholic Church, Minnesota Council on the Economic Status of Women, Todd County Social Services, Wadun County Social Services. A coproduction of University Community Video and KTCA: *Executive Producer* Sallie Fischer. *Funding* National Endowment for the Arts.

IN THE MIDST OF PLENTY offers a searching view of what it's like to be "the invisible poor" in rural America. The Kellers evoke the Joads and those anonymous families photographed by Dorothea Lange and Walker Evans during the Depression. The irony is that the Kellers live today in a land of seeming abundance. They are hard-working, proud, closely knit dairy farmers; but because they are unable to pay their medical bills, get a loan from the bank, or tithe to their church, their home, their land, and their very lives are endangered by forces over which they have little control. By looking at this family, producers Greg Pratt and Jim Gambone disclose the face of widespread rural American poverty–one-quarter of the American poor live in the

northcentral United States–along with some of the political and economic reasons for its existence. In contrast to TV programs like "The Waltons," which placed rural poverty in the past, this documentary places it discomfortingly in today's world of farm foreclosures and families without hope. (See also DAIRY QUEENS.)

Greg Pratt started his documentary career at University Community Video (UCV) producing for "Changing Channels." He has worked with Mike Hazard on A MAN WRITES TO A PART OF HIMSELF, as well as on many other UCV documentaries. He is now a staff producer for the Minneapolis CBS affiliate. Jim Gambone is a freelance filmmaker, best known for his film *Agent Orange.*

Interpolation

by Kit Fitzgerald and John Sanborn

1978. 29 min. color.
Distributors: EAI, Kitchen. Formats: ¾", VHS, Beta.

Credits: Post-produced at Synapse Video Center, Syracuse University; "Access" post-produced at Georgia State Educational Television Center for WPBT/Miami. *Funding* National Endowment for the Arts.

From their modest beginnings in 1976 with little money and an oddly ritualistic approach to video (they carted monitors through deserted downtown Manhattan streets in a manner more reminiscent of medieval penitents than avant-garde artists) Kit Fitzgerald and John Sanborn went on to discover state-of-the-art video technology, launch a new video style, and make video history by dazzling not only the art world but the people in cable and music video.

The key to their style is "visual humming," a combination of the visual vocabulary of television—rapid editing, unusual juxtapositions, and special effects—with the rhythms of new music. This produces multitextured, unconventional narratives that are as entertaining as they are provocative. Their technique, in television terms, is closest to replays of sports highlights, which focus on three or four peak moments in a game rather than the whole event. The object is to distill the work into high points so that the viewer will want to watch it over and over again.

Produced in 1978, INTERPOLATION is a sampler of short works with such enigmatic, one-word titles as "Jargon," "Motive," "Lux," and "Aphasia." "Entropy," the opening work, breaks down a linear narrative about breakfast by recombining numerous quick edits lasting as long as 30 seconds or as short as a frame (one-thirtieth of a

64

second). The result is a two minute and ten second masterwork of sensually evocative breakfast images and sounds: egg yolks running, cereal pouring into a bowl, dirty dishes piled in a sink, kitchen cabinet doors slamming, and milk plopping into a bowl. By rearranging these moments nonsequentially and repeating them at varying intervals for visual and acoustic rhythm, Fitzgerald and Sanborn reveal the essence of breakfast as experience while amusing and entertaining us with its altered reality.

The next piece, "Order," organizes seemingly random noises—a hammer pounding, a hand clapping, a glass shattering, and a bell ringing—into a symphony of found music. And in the final segment, "Access," a conventional story is transformed into a short, dynamic tale of suspense. It's a melodramatic case of corporate espionage: A trenchcoat figure skulks about a vast office, escaping with a confidential file tucked under his arm. Yet there is nothing straightforward about this tale: Events are reordered to maximize visual and aural rhythms; phones ring, doors snap shut, and a paper shredder tears up its sheets, furnishing some of the musical elements for this fast-paced puzzle.

The Irish Tapes

by John Reilly and Stefan Moore

1971–74. 56 min. b/w.
Distributors: EAI, Global Village, MDMA. Formats: ¾″, VHS, Beta.

Credits: *Editors* Stefan Moore, Jeffrey Kleinman *Interviewer* Louise Denver *Camera* Laura Adasko, Claude Beller, Louise Denver, Stefan Moore, Joel Moss, David Reedom, John Reilly, Bob Wagner *Assistants* Neil Conan, Peggy Eliot, Ken Kohl, Arby Schuman, Ray Sundlin. *Special Thanks* John and Yoko Ono Lennon *Associate Producer* Louise Denver *Producer* John Reilly. Produced in association with Global Village.

Shot mainly during the spring of 1972, this vérité-style documentary explores the troubles of Northern Ireland, contrasting Irish-American attitudes with the hard-edged reality of people living in a combat zone. An opening montage of IRA posters, armored tank carriers, and children with guns in the streets is juxtaposed with the St. Patrick's Day Parade in New York City. Interviews with paradegoers on their views of the strife in Northern Ireland reveal the confusion of apathy and anger at communist influence and British intervention. Back in the embittered six counties, children of various ages tell horror tales of men, women, and children shot down by British soldiers. Interviews with widows of IRA "freedom fighters" and families of men held in British internment camps such as Long Kesh are contrasted with statements by British officals reported on the television news.

The tape underlines the plight of Northern Ireland's Catholics, dramatically presented at an impromptu wedding where the bride and groom (who has been released from prison for a few hours) are saluted with the clanging of garbage lids, the warning signal of a raid. The Protestants are also shown suffering losses, at the Europa Hotel, target of an IRA bombing raid. The tape ends with a rather ambiguous freeze frame from a clip shown earlier—a woman shot in the face and bloody is led by two others, angry and in shock at the random violence. It is not clear whether they are Catholic or Protestant, and the producers seem to say that the violence for all must stop. Shaky camera work and more enthusiasm than precision speak of the early days of guerrilla TV, but the tape's underlying viewpoint—that the British should get out of Ireland—is clear, marking this as one of the first documentaries made in the United States in defense of this position.

THE IRISH TAPES was originally shown as a multichannel installation: Two monitors simultaneously showed contrasting images, creating a dialogue between the New York Irish merrymaking on St. Patrick's Day and Irish falling dead in the streets of Belfast. When it was aired over public television, a brief interview with the producers in the control room preserved a few moments of this unusual narrative technique to create a multilevel documentary experience.

John Reilly was one of the original founders of New York's Global Village, one of the first venues for exhibition and later, production of video in the early Seventies. Reilly, who is of Irish descent, traveled to Ireland several times with coproducer Stefan Moore to make this tape. Since then, he has worked with his wife, Julie Gustafson, on the production of a number of documentaries (see THE PURSUIT OF HAPPINESS and GIVING BIRTH) and has been a champion of independent producer's rights to air their work on public television. Stefan Moore has since teamed up with Claude Beller to produce a number of award-winning video and film documentaries (see PRESUMED INNOCENT).

It Starts at Home

by Michael Smith

1982. 25 min. color.
Distributors: EAI, Kitchen, Video Data Bank. Format: ¾".

Credits: *Director* Mark Fischer *Producers* Michael Smith, Mark Fischer *Script* Mark Fischer, Carole Ann Klonarides, Michael Smith.

IT STARTS AT HOME is a new wave sitcom, a send-up of the genre, featuring Mike Blandman, a sympathetic comic victim in the tradition of Keaton and Chaplin. Bland Mike is performance artist Michael Smith's alter ego. He has had cable installed in his apartment.

Wandering about in his underwear—oversized boxer shorts, T-shirt, and socks with garters—Mike switches on the set only to discover something very odd: Somehow his TV has turned into a camera, and millions of viewers are watching him on their sets. He approaches his TV tentatively, from oblique angles, peering at his own face looking back at him from the screen. Like a primitive confronted with a photo of himself, he regards the image fearfully, suspiciously, incredulously. In a snap, a fast-talking producer named Bob (who is portrayed as a ratlike toupee) sizes up the situation and hurries over to sign him up. Calling him "Baby" and "Mikela," Bob promises to make Mike a star. But Mike has his own ideas, and he tries out a number of routines: an Egyptian sidestep appropriate to the medium's two-dimensional reality and an Astaire-like number in top hat, white tie, and tails. Not surprisingly, Mike's timing is far from Astaire's, but in his innocence, he hardly notices. His television viewers hardly care.

Like Chauncey in Jerzy Kosinski's *Being There,* Mike is a victim of television. His passivity and dullness and his reactive behavior define him as a TV viewer. When the medium suddenly turns into a surveillance camera, exposing him in his underwear for all the world to see, it is unexpected but not that surprising. He adapts, exchanging his boring reality for the glamorous images of past glories, whether dynastic ancient Egypt or as screen god Fred Astaire. Mike never climbs out of his own muddled middle-class self. Meanwhile, behind the deadpan mask, Smith turns the medium inside out to poke fun at our preoccupation with the boob tube and all it signifies.

L.A. Nickel

by Branda Miller

1983. 9 min. color.
Distributors: EAI, Video Data Bank. Formats: ¾″, VHS, Beta.

Credits: *Original Soundtrack* The Doo-Dooettes (Tom Recchion, Fredrik Nilsen) *Art Director* Jeff Isaak *Camera* Marcel Shain, Gordon Metcalfe, Ante Bozanich, Michael Intriere, Gary Wong, Nick Ursin *Creative Consultant/Production Coordinator* Steve Silas *Installation Technician* Stuart Bender *Installation Color Camera* Marcel Shain *Video/Cinema Consultants* Bob Diva, John Ten Hoor *Live Sound Design* Rick Fine *"Audio Agents" on Street* Judy Bozanich, Jeff Isaak, Roxanna Lohse, Tim Malloy, Chuck Roche, Margret Von Biesen *Edited* L.B.M.A. Video. *"I'm Too Fucked Up/5 Cent Lament": Emulator Consultant* David Bradshaw *Audio Engineer* Paul Cutler. Recorded at Ricky Nix Control Center Studios.

Using a surveillance camera, video artist Branda Miller recorded a skid row hangout in downtown Los Angeles, surveying the last mo-

ments of activity before urban development disbanded the area, which has been called the city's central "hotbed of decay." L.A. NICK-EL's opening scenes are rapid edits cut to a complex music track devised by synthesizing the street sounds of jackhammers, police sirens, helicopter propellers, and the assorted mutterings of the bums, pimps, prostitutes, and drunks who loiter on the street. The sound is so abstracted it has become the heartbeat of this skid row dive, a staccato rhythm that twitches as the camera jerks, plunging closer for a view of a fight. The fragmented, hallucinatory quality of the Doo-Dooettes score, "I'm Too Fucked Up," fuses with the restlessly searching camera and comes to personify the fragmented consciousness of this derelict quarter.

Night falls, times passes, and the scene changes, as lush, romantic music swells in the background. In a dreamy haze, lights stream by in dizzying curves: headlights of a police car touring the streets and blinking neon signs that resemble a drunken scrawl. Light replaces the ragged tattoo of the first half of the tape with its own more fluid visual pulse. This "5-Cent Lament" is both seductive and sinister, a drunken dream about illusion, a glimpse of yet another ring of hell. It is interrupted by a reprise of an incoherent male voice from earlier, as we cruise to a stop before a red light and pan up to see the outline of the Hard Rock Café.

Miller, an Emmy-winning editor, creates a surreal landscape of urban despair that lingers in the mind long after the tape has ended. Her densely textured work plunges beneath surfaces, unearthing some profound and disturbing visual and aural equivalents for a living death.

The Lord of the Universe

by Top Value Television (TVTV)

1974. 60 min. b/w & color.
Distributor: EAI. Formats: ¾″, VHS, Beta.

Credits: TVTV: Hudson Marquez, Allen Rucker, Michael Shamberg, Tom Weinberg, Megan Williams *Production* Wendy Appel, Skip Blumberg, Bill Bradbury, John Brumage, Steve Christiansen, Paul Goldsmith, Stanton Kaye, John Keeler, Anda Korsts, Harry Mathias, Doug Michels, Tom Morey, Rita Ogden, Tom Richmond, Van Schley, Jody Sibert, Elon Soltes, Akio Yamaguchi *Editing* Wendy Appel, Hudson Marquez, Rita Ogden, Allen Rucker, Michael Shamberg, Elon Soltes. *Thanks* Tom Morey and Video Sales Inc., Houston; Marilyn Lubetkin, Pierre Jouchmans, K.A.F. Inc., Allen Kaplan, Location Video Services, Shri Hans Productions, Bruce Stanford, Technisphere. Produced in association with the Television Lab at WNET/13: *Supervising Editor* John J. Godfrey *Assistant Editor* Philip Falcone *Production Manager* Darlene Mastro *Assistant to Producer* Diane English *Production Secretary* Lynn Hott *Executive Producer* David Loxton. *Funding* The Stern Fund, The Corporation for Public Broadcasting, The Vanguard Foundation.

Awards: Dupont-Columbia Journalism Award.

The first independent video documentary made for national broadcast on public television, THE LORD OF THE UNIVERSE is an exposé of the Guru Maharaj Ji and his Millenium '73 gathering at the Houston Astrodome. TVTV's crew of 24 covered the preparations for what the guru billed as "the central event in human history." One crew followed a devotee from his home in Brooklyn to Houston, while other crews interviewed guards, astrologers, premies (followers of the guru), mahatmas (priests), and the "Holy Family," as well as Sixties radicals Rennie Davis and Abbie Hoffman. Having traded in his role as radical political leader for that of spokesman for an improbable religion, Davis sings the guru's praises while Hoffman, watching him on tape, comments on his former colleague's arrogance and skills as a propagandist. "It's different saying you've found God, than saying you know his address and credit card number," Hoffman quips, emphasizing the materialism of this guru's religion.

Switching back and forth between the preparations for and actual on-stage performances of the 15-year-old guru, cameras focus on blissed-out devotees, pathetically seeking stability and guidance in the guru's fold. Neon lights, glitter, rock music furnished by the guru's brother (a rotund clone of Elvis Presley), and a Las Vegas stage set are the guru's accoutrements as he gives *satsang* (discourse on knowledge) to his faded flower-children followers. Outside, angry arguments between premies and Hare Krishna followers and a militant, Bible-spouting fundamentalist expose the undercurrent of violence, repression, and control in extremist religions. One burly bodyguard sums it up neatly: "I don't have to think. I have knowledge."

At a press conference that frustrates reporters, one woman asks insistently what became of the reporter who threw a cream pie at the guru. Maharaj Ji's flippancy switches to petulance at the question. Pat Haley, the journalist prankster, is interviewed elsewhere, describing how a mahatma and premie beat him and smashed his skull so badly that he required a metal plate. Veiled violence pervades the tape and is almost palpable in the air.

Our Brooklyn devotee, Michael, finally gets "the Knowledge," and we, too, learn the four secret meditation techniques (light, music, nectar, word) courtesy of ex-premies who express their disillusionment with the guru and his materialism. Hoffman has the last word when he says, "If this guy is God, this is the God the United States deserves!" Concluding the tape is a crawl with information on the guru's million-dollar assets and far-flung financial holdings.

Much in evidence here is TVTV's creative use of graphics, live music, and wide-angle-lens shots to convey the desperate efforts of these lost children to find a leader and their exploitation by this religious fake. As always, there is humor to leaven the situation. At one point, Michael innocently says, "I don't know whether it's the air conditioning, but you can really feel something." But the humor is black humor in the end, and the lingering image is of one poor soul giggling madly, with one of the guru's discarded flowers clasped to his lips. THE LORD OF THE UNIVERSE is a sharp, ground-breaking inside look at cult behavior presented in an entertaining, if chilling, way. TVTV, at home in the world of spectacle and carnival, ever agile in debunking power seekers, succeeds admirably in producing an award-winning documentary that remains timely. (See also FOUR MORE YEARS.)

The Love Tapes, Series 18

by Wendy Clarke

1981. 58 min. b/w.
Distributor: EAI. Formats: ¾", VHS, Beta.

Credits: Produced through Kineholistics.

THE LOVE TAPES is an amazing series of self-revelations by people of all ages and walks of life speaking about love. It opens with a voice-over explanation by Clarke of how each three-minute tape was made, followed by 15 samples. By turns funny, pained, angry, contented, philosophic, sensitive, and weird, these statements offer striking commentary on the complexity and endurance of love today. A young black teen says, "Love is like these sunglasses: I send love out, but I'm afraid for other people to love me. . . . I'm going to tell you a secret: I'm afraid of people—of getting hurt." A pretty blond teen gushes over her current love, carefully appending a final remark, "I want to be with him for as long as I can . . . while it's still good." A disabled Japanese man speaks of his discovery of love as a child, concluding, "Love makes it possible to open the heart closed by fear of rejection." A black musician, "God's choice cellist," says he loves to get hurt because it makes him play better. And a young Hispanic man begins shyly, "Love does exist in New York City, in me. Love me, I'm lovable! Will anyone say that they love me?" A divorced father speaks about his fierce love for his son, and a teenage boy explains how he was in bad shape, fighting in gangs, beating up teachers: "I never knew what love was until I met my [foster] family." A little girl ends the tape, softly thinking aloud, "Well, I love stuffed animals. Or maybe I love myself or maybe I could love my life?"

Clarke's campaign, enlisting over 800 people across the country—prison inmates, museum visitors, battered women, the disabled, among many others—yields inspiring, disturbing, and provocative glimpses of who we are and how we feel. Most critics have hailed this interactive video art—part portrait, part autobiography—as a celebration of love, although one found it a sign of the alienation "at the base of contemporary social interactions in America." Wendy Clarke has worked in video since the early Seventies, when she began her video journals, the inspiration for this more-than-five-year-long project. She was a member of the T. P. Videospace Troupe, an experimental art group organized by her mother, film- and video-maker Shirley Clarke. THE LOVE TAPES has been broadcast on public television and shown in museums and libraries around the country.

Low 'N Slow, The Art of Lowriding

by Rick Tejada-Flores

1983. 29 min. color.
Distributor: Alturas Films. Formats: ¾", VHS, Beta.

Credits: *Camera* Lewis Wensk *Audio* Mark Berger *Production Coordinator* Patrice O'Neill *Additional Audio* Wolf Seeburg, David Dobkin *Animation Design* Rupert Garcia *Animation Director* Kathryn Lenihan *Title Song* Jorge Santana *Mix* Steve Pinsky.

Lowriding is more than just an automobile fetish; it's a vivid expression of Chicano culture and pride. Fantastically painted cars are equipped with hydraulic pumps so that they can travel close to the ground for low 'n slow cruising in Chicano communities throughout

the Southwest. In this lively, upbeat, visually opulent tape, Rick Tejada-Flores traces lowriding's roots back to the zoot suit era of the Twenties and beyond to the traditional Latin *paseo,* or promenade. He interviews some of the many people who constitute the world of lowriding: *chollos,* or car-club members, artists who decorate hoods and mechanics who customize chassis, DJs who broadcast on lowrider radio stations and writers at *Low Rider* magazine, and parents and clergy who support their lowriding children. They explain how these elaborately painted, customized cars celebrate beauty and Hispanic identity.

For an Anglo culture that emphasizes getting someplace fast, lowriders seem to flout social as well as civil laws. In California, where hydraulic pumps that permit cars to hop like bucking horses are illegal, clubs have been banned from public streets. In response to such cultural misunderstandings, Tejada- Flores's tape reveals the ethnic context that makes lowriding a mark of prestige and a sign of manhood in Chicano culture. LOW 'N SLOW is as entertaining as it is illuminating.

A Man Writes to a Part of Himself: The Poetry of Robert Bly

by Mike Hazard and Greg Pratt

1978. 58 min. color.
Distributor: UCVideo. Formats: ¾″, VHS, Beta.

Credits: *Producer/Writer/Editor* Greg Pratt, Mike Hazard *Executive Producer* Stephen Kulczycki *Associate Producer* Paul Burtness

Narrator Tom McGrath *Camera* Greg Pratt *2d Camera* Jim Mulligan *Additional Camera* Paul Burtness *Sound* David Brown, John Velie, Mike Hazard, Jan Folstad, Jean Marie Ziegler *Production Assistants* Bob Timm, Pat Olson, Rick Snider *Graphics* Cats Pajamas. *Funding* Minnesota State Arts Board, National Endowment for the Arts.

Awards: Gold Hugo, Chicago Film Festival; Silver Plaque, Athens Video Festival; Input.

This beautiful, affecting portrait of poet Robert Bly links the man and his art to his roots in rural Minnesota. As we see him splitting wood in the snow and riding a tractor on his farm with one of his four children astride his knees, he expresses his belief in hard work and grounding oneself in the earth "near where you were born." Bly is interviewed in the library of his lakeside cabin in northern Minnesota; he is seen reading his poems to an appreciative audience in an old church; and he is shown reveling at a gathering of friends, where he reads poems, tells stories, and chants while playing a dulcimer. He speaks about the importance of discovering his "feminine," or feeling, side and reads the poem that gives the tape its title.

It was not until he was in the navy during World War II that Bly first heard a poem, and he credits this event with his first inspiration to write. Years later, the war in Vietnam inspired him to write poetry against the war, thrusting him into the public consciousness and winning him both acclaim and derision. Glimpsed between his candid disclosures about the nature of poetry and politics in art, videomakers Pratt and Hazard present beautiful Minnesotan scenes at a lyrical pace to accompany the resonant voice of the narrator, poet Tom McGrath, filling in the background of Bly's life and career. This tape is about a man, a poet, and a way of looking at the world and living fully; it is one of the best examples of translating poetry into a visual medium.

Greg Pratt, an alumnus of University Community Video in Minneapolis, has been producing video documentaries since the early Seventies and has since become a staff producer for the Minneapolis CBS affiliate. This tape is part of a series produced by Mike Hazard on Minnesota writers: "Poets & Writers in Motion." The series includes profiles of poet Tom McGrath and novelist Frederick Manfred (see AMERICAN GRIZZLY).

Mayday Realtime

by David Cort

1970. 60 min. b/w.
Distributor: EAI. Formats: ¾″, VHS, Beta.

Credits: *Editing/Post-production Facilities* Electronic Arts Intermix.

One of the earliest uses of portable video was to document the complex social world of the late Sixties and early Seventies—from love-ins to antiwar demonstrations. MAYDAY REALTIME has a bit of both. David Cort—a founding member of the Videofreex, one of the best-known early video collectives—took his black-and-white Portapak to Washington, DC, to record his impressions of the historic 1970 May Day antiwar rally. The tape is a period piece, a rambling, haphazard "happening" of a documentary, shot out of the front seat of a car prowling about Washington before and during the demonstration. Cort later moved onto the streets following protesters running away from Mace-carrying police and finally hid away in an idyllic glen inhabited by hippie women and children.

Cort expresses the gritty reality of confusion, the instant comradeship, and the often shrill desperation of the antiwar years, a time of high purpose that often culminated in getting high. From the car radio come news reports explaining what is happening, where the blockades are, where the police are spraying Mace. Leaning out of the car, Cort shouts warnings to protesters and engages passersby in casual interviews about their opinions of what is going on. Once the action has heated up, with people lying in the street trying to block-ade traffic and helicopters hovering in the air, the tape moves ab-ruptly to a bucolic landscape where children are skipping stones across a stream. John Lennon's song "Power to the People" hangs in the air while Cort talks about his divorce to his companions, who, stoned on marijuana, laughingly take turns holding the camera. One woman hands the camera to a child, and the closing shots of abrupt, random camera play seem to call for a return to simplicity and innocence, rounding out the romantic vision that underlies the work.

It is a rough tape, edited in the camera when editing was still a primitive process, a fact that led to a new aesthetic of better— unmanipulated "real-time" tapes, going direct cinema one or worse, depending on your point of view. Since few early videomakers were trained in film or television, the visual qualities and sense of narra-tive development were frequently crude: dirty lenses, images out of focus, odd jumps in continuity characterized much early work. These pioneers were determined to come up with their own forms, different from work designed for television or films. They brought to their work a vitality and raw energy that held the seeds of what would later prove to be a revolutionary approach to news and documentary coverage, the "live news" or "action news" which has since become a familiar part of every nightly newscast. MAYDAY REALTIME embodies the best and the worst of early "guerrilla television."

Cort was a major figure in the early East Coast video scene, often dominating it with his manic laughter, his wild curly black hair, and his high-pitched energy. Moving with the Videofreex to Lanesville, NY, he became part of the group's transition to Media Bus, one of the first community-based video groups and the first to transmit their programs via low-power TV. Trained as an actor, Cort was largely interested in the dramatic and interactive possibilities of video, creating video games that exploited the electronic wizardry of the technology. He continues to teach courses in video in the Boston area.

Media Burn

by Ant Farm

1975. 25 min. color.
Distributor: EAI, MOMA. Formats: ¾″, VHS, Beta.

Credits: Ant Farm: Chip Lord, Doug Michels, Curtis Schreier, Uncle Buddie *Executive Producer* Tom Weinberg *Artist-President* Doug Hall *Friends* Dan Calderwood, Marie Ford, Ceil Cruesing, Diane Hall,

John Hilding, Phil Makanna, The Residents, Edmund Shea, Starr Sutherland, T.R. Uthco, Judith Williams *Video Production* Optic Nerve: Lynn Adler, Jules Backus, Jim Mayer, Sherrie Rabinowitz, John Rodgers, Mya Shone; Marin County Video: Burt Aronowitz, Robert Keller, John Gillette; California Video Resource Project: Craig Schiller, Will Hoover, Jay Braunstein, E.C., John Hunt. Plus: T.L. Morey, David Cort, William Farley, Chuck Koteen, KCRA-TV. *Editors* Chip Lord, Skip Blumberg, Doug Michels, Tom Weinberg. Edited at Lanesville TV, NY, and Synapse, Syracuse University: Lance Wisniewski, Paul Dougherty, Lisa Seidenberg, Dean Leeson. *Phantom Dream Car* Uncle Buddie's Used Cars. *Funding* National Endowment for the Arts and New York State Council on the Arts.

MEDIA BURN is media criticism at its most imaginative. The tape contrasts commercial television's news coverage and Ant Farm's own report of an art happening the group sponsored to highlight the media's role in staging and manipulating events as news. The tape opens with a montage of commercial TV news coverage for the Fourth of July, 1975: traffic fatalities, fireworks, Bob Hope being awarded the freedom medal at Independence Hall. Then the anchorperson for "Action News" reports:

> A media event is something that happens only because somebody made it happen . . . only because somebody figures the TV news cameras would show up to watch it happen. (It used to be called a publicity stunt.) Today some people decided to stage what they call the *ultimate* media event. . . .

The scene shifts to "Action News" reporter David Louie:

> It had nothing to do with the Fourth of July. . . . [It was] an art and culture happening called "Media Burn" by members of an art group driving a modified 1959 Cadillac through a pyramid of burning TV sets—their way of alleviating the frustration of watching TV. . . . Even though the artists were knocking TV, they were using it to make their point.

No media event is complete without a central figure, a VIP to give credibility to the event. The media-conscious sponsors resurrected John F. Kennedy for the keynote speech. . . . The formalities over, they poured kerosene over and under the TV sets and set them ablaze. That set the stage for the media burn. Two daredevil drivers in the tradition of Evel Knievel settled into the crash car and took off. . . . The car, or what's left of it, is now up for sale. The organization which sponsored this event was Ant Farm. What other organization would make a mountain out of a molehill? It may not be good art in some people's minds, but at least it was good entertainment.

Louie's report is a conventional, seamless voice-over interpretation of a soft-news event; his commentary is heard over a rapid montage of images: souvenir sellers, people eating hotdogs, video

cameras, the artist-president at his TV podium, and finally the crash. The only live sound is the smack of the car on impact and background noises over Louie's on-site sign-off. There is nothing of the Kennedy-esque speech, no interviews of the crowd, no comments by the organizers. Louie mediates the event and provides an editorial punchline put-down for his ending. Next is a clip from KPIX-TV: "If smashing a 1959 Cadillac into a wall of TV sets is art, then the world may rest tonight with a new masterpiece. If it is culture, then perhaps we're all in a degree of difficulty not previously experienced in this society." A sidekick remarks: "Now that is weird. I think it's over our heads." A WTVU-TV reporter concludes his coverage with this: "What's it all mean? Well, presumably, the message is for the media, get it?" Back in the studio, the anchorperson replies, "I don't think I want to get it."

In contrast to this, Ant Farm then offers its own funky but thorough coverage of "Media Burn." Interviews include a woman at the souvenir stand who says, "I see this event as highlighting the themes of violence on TV." The camera pans around the crowd, taking in the arrival of the artist-president. Mimicking Kennedy's vocal and rhetorical style, he addresses the crowd from his podium, an enormous TV set:

> Members of the press, my fellow Americans . . . Television, because of its technology and the way it is used, can only produce autocratic political forms and hopeless alienation. Who can deny

we are a nation addicted to TV and the constant flow of mass media?. . .

Concluding by saying, "The world may never understand what is done here today but the image will never be forgotten," the artist-president leaves, replaced by "media matadors" dressed in white suits and helmets that vividly recall astronauts at a space launch. They climb on top of the Phantom Dream Car and stand at attention as the national anthem is played. As they enter the vehicle through the roof, a closed-circuit camera inside shows them attaching the protective shields that are designed to seal out all light. Their rebuilt car is equipped with Video-Vision—a closed-circuit video camera mounted on top of the car, which will serve as the driver's "image-seeking guidance system." When all systems check out, the car takes off and crashes through the bank of 50 burning TV sets. This scene is re-viewed from different angles, instant replays—including slow-motion—taken from television sports. The drivers emerge from the car unscathed, having "kicked the TV habit." After they are paraded around the parking lot of the San Francisco Cow Palace in ticker-tape-hero fashion, Ant Farm's coverage closes with a speeded-up replay of the crash, showing people scurrying about like ants, as television statistics appear superimposed over the scene.

MEDIA BURN brilliantly contrasts the conventions of TV news with an alternate version of a media event. The snide, silly, even defensive remarks of the TV newspeople protect them and their audience from the message of media burning. The very content of the media burn event is a parody of American culture as brought to you by television. John F. Kennedy, the first president to be elected and buried via television, is a wonderfully ironic choice to speak out on media control. Along with political speeches and sporting events, Ant Farm satirizes as media events the space launches of the Sixties and the annual unveiling of the latest in automotive engineering. Playfully, entertainingly, they address a macho American fascination with destruction, domination, power, and information control. By asking the question "Haven't you ever wanted to put your foot through your television set?," Ant Farm ultimately asks viewers to question their own passivity as TV viewers.

Ant Farm was a San Francisco collective of artists and architects that, from 1968 to 1978, staged a number of happenings and produced several tapes, including *The Eternal Frame* and *The Cadillac Ranch Show.*

Meta Mayan II

by Edin Velez

1981. 20 min. color.
Distributors: EAI, MOMA. Formats: ¾″, VHS, Beta.

Credits: *Producers* Ethel Velez and Edin Velez *Production Assistant* Amy Rosmarin *Associate Director* Eulogio Ortiz, Jr. *Videotape Editor* Scott Doniger *Electronic Graphics* Rand Joseph. *Thanks* Henry Bornstein, Ted Estabrook, Amnesty International, Leonard Akimbo, MPCS Video Inc., Larry Hapit, Alan Neil. Produced in association with the Television Lab at WNET/13: *Post-production Coordinator* Barbara Ravis *Executive Producer* Carol Brandenburg. *Funding* New York State Council on the Arts, The Jerome Foundation, National Endowment for the Arts, Creative Artists Public Service Program.

In META MAYAN II, Edin Velez exaggerates the cultural rhythms of the mountain Indians of northern Guatemala, revealing the depth of their culture and their conflict with a hostile outside world. The tape opens and closes with the same woman walking down a country road, looking with grave suspicion, veiled anger, and grudging curiosity at the camera. The stark beauty of her dark, furrowed brows and her walk, suspended in slow motion, become an emblem of the Indians' seriousness and vulnerability. Like her, they are suspended in time and space. The drone of the American news report of fighting among the peasants (i.e., Indians) violates the quiet that embraces her slowly walking figure and announces the danger surrounding her.

Seen also in slow motion are men and boys, clothed in medieval-looking robes and walking in a religious procession. It is not clear whether the great float they bear on their shoulders is a source of oppression or a ritual bond that holds them and their world together. This ambiguity leaves the viewer room for speculation and involvement. What is clear is the earnest dignity of their faces, young and old alike.

In sharp contrast with their stately, cadenced walk comes a dizzying pan of the marketplace, a riot of bright colors streaming like a rainbow from brilliant embroidered clothing. The market is alive with a life that is somehow speeding past its own inhabitants.

Throughout the tape, Velez threads images of the four elements: Woven like the bright colors of a Guatemalan embroidery are scenes of women staring into fires or washing clothes in a river; encircling all is a magnificent 360° sweep of sky and mountains that inscribes the Guatemalan land and spirit. Over this the words from the *Popol Vuh* appear: "This is the story of how it began, all calm, in silence, and the sky was empty." Out of Velez's respect for the mystery, grace, and integrity of the Indians and their endangered culture he fashions a striking visual equivalent of the complex forces at work within and outside their world.

Velez's impulse as a documentarist is more poetic than reformist, resembling the epic quest of Robert Flaherty in *Nanook of the North* to extol the nobility of the Inuits and their vanishing way of life. In META MAYAN II Velez focuses not on the warfare or destruction threatening these Indians but on their dignity and well-founded mistrust of outsiders. Because he avoids the hard-line stance of leftist documentaries, eschewing literalism and agit-prop techniques for a personal approach that employs image manipulation and a nonnarrative structure, META MAYAN II is often viewed more as video art than documentary. Velez's answer is to call his tapes "video essays," avoiding categories that seem to limit rather than reveal the richness and subtlety of his work.

Born in Puerto Rico, Velez was trained as a painter, but he left his brushes and his home in the late Sixties for the new medium of video. In New York City, he spent several years making abstract expressionist tapes, using video synthesizers and colorizers, but was dissatisfied with his inability to discover feeling in his images. He then turned to the documentary mode and his cultural roots. His first color documentary was the award-winning *Tule: The Cuna Indians of San Blas,* a richly textured tape about Panamanian Indians who live in self-imposed isolation to maintain their centuries-old traditions. Since META MAYAN II, Velez has produced a portrait of new-music composer Brian Eno, OBLIQUE STRATEGIST TOO, and *As Is,* Velez's personal vision of New York City.

Montana

by Jane Veeder

1982. 3 min. color.
Distributor: MOMA. Format: ¾".

In this award-winning tape, Chicago-based video artist Jane Veeder uses ZGRASS, a computer graphics language designed by Tom DeFanti for use with the Sandin Image Processor. She presents the great outdoors in the graphic terms of an electronic video game, drawing on the aesthetics of the game's sounds and symbols for her tableaux of buffalo, eagles, craggy mountains, globes, wheat, thunderbolts, and video cameras that race across the screen like decoys in a video arcade shooting gallery. She aurally confounds both real and electronic space, mixing bird chirps and a recitation of bird names with the well-known electronic beeps and grunts of arcade games.

Designed for display on a TV monitor, this tape could easily be shown on a football stadium scoreboard or an electronic billboard: The two-dimensional figures and their messages are perfectly suited to such low-definition, symbolic communication systems. Veeder's MONTANA cleverly parodies the video game, offering a playful yet potentially sobering view of America's last frontier, where we are all invited to have "Good Luck Electronically Visualizing Your Future."

Monterey's Boat People

by Spencer Nakasako and Vincent Digirolamo

1982. 29 min. color.
Distributor: Spencer Nakasako. Formats: ¾″, VHS, Beta.

Credits: *Director of Photography* Michael Chin *Production Manager* Steven Brudnick *Post-production Sound* Curtis Choy *CMX Editor* Lo Mack *Music* Hiroshima.

Awards: Red Ribbon, American Film Festival.

In this beautifully photographed documentary, Spencer Nakasako and Vincent Digirolamo investigate the problems, past and present, of Asian fishermen in California's Monterey Bay. They open by carefully tracing the history of prejudice dating back to 1853, when Chinese fishermen first developed Monterey as a major fishing area, going on to focus on the problems of Vietnamese and Koreans, whose controversial fishing with monofilament gill nets has stirred up the ire of Italian boat owners, captains of the market and the seas. Using a straightforward journalistic style, the producers elicit sensitive interviews that expose the complex tangle of issues—conservation concerns, economic competition, and racial prejudice—that face Monterey's boat people.

MOVE: Confrontation in Philadelphia

by Jane Mancini and Karen Pomer

1980. 60 min. b/w.
Distributor: Temple University. Formats: ¾″, VHS.
Awards: Blue Ribbon, American Film Festival; Perspectives in Community Television.

This is an investigative report on the 1978 eviction of a radical black political commune in Philadelphia by Mayor Frank Rizzo. Billed by the media as a back-to-nature group, MOVE was a highly complex entity, and producers Jane Mancini and Karen Pomer document the intricate relationships of media bias, police harassment, and subtle economic motivation that led to MOVE's violent removal by the police in August 1978.

Shifting from newspaper headlines to television newscasts, from mayoral press conferences to on-the-street interviews with community residents, Mancini and Pomer reveal how the media manipulated the news and how the black community in Philadelphia proved to be a pawn in a political and media chess game.

Far from the smooth, controlled television aesthetic, here is shaky camera work, dizzying swish pans, and choppy editing. There is no correspondent to cool down the events by fitting them into a predictable format overladen with continuous, controlling commentary. Instead, there are Pomer and Mancini, students when they began the tape as a class project. Spending two-and-a-half years on the project, shooting more than 50 hours of tape, they were able to follow the story to its bloody climax. Turning what might otherwise have been serious limitations to their advantage, the two young women made their youth, inexperience, and unintimidating presence with small-format video equipment work for them, gaining the trust not only of the black community and MOVE supporters but also of the local media. The rough and jagged quality of their images grippingly communicates the raw immediacy of a volatile situation. This is an exceptional example of how the early "street video" style and commitment survived into the Seventies. By providing detailed background on MOVE's origins and philosophy, it adds historic perspective and helps explain the 1985 MOVE confrontation, where police bombed a MOVE house, destroying by fire several city blocks of a middle-class black community in Philadelphia.

My Father Sold Studebakers

by Skip Sweeney

1983. 28 min. color.
Distributor: Video Free America. Formats: ¾″, VHS, Beta.

Credits: *Producer/Writer/Editor* Skip Sweeney *Coproducer* Joanne Kelly. A coproduction of Video Free America and the Television Lab at WNET/13: *Executive Producer* Carol Brandenburg.

Awards: Atlanta Film & Video Festival, Tyneside Film Festival.

Part family portrait, part autobiography, part dialogue with a lost father, MY FATHER SOLD STUDEBAKERS is Skip Sweeney's bumpy journey down memory lane in pursuit of understanding and reconciliation with his dad. It opens with loving camera caresses of the star-billed car, kept in ace condition by young Sweeney. Ray Sweeney was indeed a Studebaker salesman, and for a long time the car was about the only thing Skip liked about his father. Unexpectedly, we see an old black-and-white tape of a funeral: The casket is lifted out of a hearse in slow motion as Skip explains that when his father died, he was relieved that he would never have to see his disapproving face again. But when Skip's own son was born, he saw once again in the wrinkled, scowling face of his newborn his father's face. He knew then that he finally had to come to terms with the father who had thrown him out of the house at 19 for having long hair.

Sweeney, who has been making videotapes since the late Sixties, used his personal archive of tapes and family movies to uncover the layers of his past, enlisting his mother and brother and sisters in a sort of video encounter session to discover what the family thought of Ray and his relationship with Skip. As they talk, teasing and laugh-

ing, they end up revealing more about themselves than intended, and we discover in Skip the shy kid who always "wanted attention, then forgot what he wanted to say."

It isn't until Skip talks to the guys who worked for Ray in the Studebaker dealership that all the pieces fall in place. Ray treated everyone alike—his workers as well as children. "His father kicked his ass, so he kicked our ass," one fellow bluntly states. At 50, Ray Sr. was still dominated by *his* father. He couldn't cope with Skip's problems at puberty, the mechanic says, because he couldn't cope with his own: getting away from his own father. Skip had, in his own words, made the "flip-flop from being an altar boy to a human being," having discovered sex, not surprisingly, in the back seat of a Studebaker. Skip's father—who couldn't break away from his own father's control—couldn't abide his son's independence and rebelliousness. Conflict was inevitable.

Purged of anger and confusion, Skip leaves flowers at his father's grave, but in a more highly symbolic act of reconciliation, he shaves off his beard and cuts his hair, revealing the grinning face of his father underneath.

MY FATHER SOLD STUDEBAKERS reaches beyond the particulars of this California family and the rebellion of the late Sixties to embrace the timeless battle between fathers and sons. The tape speaks eloquently of how understanding and forgiveness can be achieved beyond the grave; it celebrates the maturity of mourning and the continuity of the generations. The first in a proposed series of family tapes, it reaches beyond self-indulgence to understand the struggle for love, acceptance, and understanding every family endures.

Sweeney, once known as the "King of Video Feedback," was a cofounder of Video Free America, a San Francisco center for video production and exhibition. Early in his pioneering video career, he developed video installations for such theater productions as Heathcote Williams's *AC/DC* and Allen Ginsberg's *Kaddish*. With his former partner, Arthur Ginsberg, he helped produce *The Continuing Story of Carel and Ferd,* a video prototype for the TV series "An American Family," which focused on the lifestyle and marriage of an oddly matched couple. Sweeney has since worked with his wife, Joanne Kelly, in making video dance tapes, video art, and, most recently, documentaries. MY FATHER SOLD STUDEBAKERS is arguably his best work.

Oblique Strategist Too

by Edin Velez

1984. 12 min. color.
Distributor: EAI. Formats: ¾", VHS, Beta.

Credits: *Producers* Ethel and Edin Velez *Location Engineer* Arby *Audio/VTR* Ethel Velez. Edited at Matrix Video: *Videotape Editor* Rick Feist *Additional Editing* International Production Center: *Videotape Editor* Frank Markward *Electronic Graphics* Patricia Megumi Ido *Post-production Audio* Video Tracks *Engineer* Chris Tergesen. *Thanks* Henry Bornstein, Alan Neil, Nina Wever, 185 Corporation, Alex Blair, J. T. Ottens, 39 Street Studio, Kip Kaplan, Bert Brander, Howard Ellis, Vincent Verpo, Iana Velez. Produced in association with the Television Lab at WNET/13: *Executive Producer* Carol Brandenburg. *Funding* New York State Council on the Arts.

OBLIQUE STRATEGIST TOO is an unconventional portrait of an unconventional composer, Brian Eno. Velez opens the tape with a quotation from Heraclitus about the nature of things being in the habit of concealing themselves, providing a gloss on the title and a clue to Velez's method as well. The tape's central image is Eno composing at an instrument panel while computer- generated, abstracted musical symbols are superimposed over him. Layer upon layer of these symbols build a dense visual texture paralleling the audio textures Eno is simultaneously creating. A slow dissolve to a close-up image of desert-pink sand dunes against a blue sky pulls out as Eno's voice explains that he is not thinking of music but of trying to create a sense of place using only sound.

Later, Eno appears in Italy giving a lecture, sweating like an inmate of Dante's Inferno, as Velez cross-cuts to a black female body builder with the legend "Disconnect from Desire" superimposed on

her glistening muscles. The apparent visual discontinuity sends one back to Eno, examining him more carefully in his impatient, arrogant relationship to the Italian audience. Back again in his studio, he speaks aloud and then smugly sucks on a pipe, as his recorded voice continues his self-absorbed monologue. "The mind makes connections between things not usually connected," he says. In commenting on our natural inclination to organize perception into meaningful patterns, he seems to beg the question of whether the randomness of his music is artful or artless.

Spare in its 12-minute duration, OBLIQUE STRATEGIST TOO has a structure that appears to be as deliberately random and calculated as Eno's music. Velez was drawn to Eno as a subject by his music, which Velez frequently played while editing his tapes, drawing from the repetitive, circular structures and richly evocative nature of Eno's compositions for the shaping of his own work. Velez produced an earlier version of the tape that was a much more conventional documentary homage rather than a collaboration, but then was unexpectedly refused the music rights. Thrown back upon himself, Velez refashioned the portrait into OBLIQUE STRATEGIST TOO, a much more artistic equivalent to Eno's complex music and an unvarnished glimpse of the man. (See also META MAYAN II.)

Ohio to Giverny: Memory of Light

by Mary Lucier

1983. 19 min. color.
Distributor: Mary Lucier. Format: ¾″.

Credits: *Audio Post-production/Music* Earl Howard *Production Assistant* Lisa Rinzler *Videotape Editor* Ann Woodward *Special Assistance* JVC Company of America. *Thanks* Versailles Foundation, Inc., Musée Claude Monet, Bucyrus Historical Society, The Kitchen, Margaret Glosser. Produced in association with the Television Lab at WNET/13: *Executive Producer* Carol Brandenburg. *Funding* New York State Council on the Arts, Jerome Foundation.

OHIO TO GIVERNY: MEMORY OF LIGHT is the single-channel version of Lucier's highly acclaimed installation for seven monitors, *Ohio at Giverny*. In this beautiful, lyrical exploration of light and memory, Lucier traces her personal and artistic roots. The tape opens with her earliest sensual memories of life on a bucolic Ohio farm. Light streaming through the window of a Victorian bedroom dances on curtains and ignites a crystal chandelier. Lucier's camera moves dynamically, darting about space with the rapid eye motions of dreaming or childhood curiosity. Rotating her camera to unexpected angles, she makes light the object of her memory, transforming the familiar into elements magical, lambent, unknown. Environmental sounds—a cow lowing, insects buzzing in the fields, wind rippling glass chimes, breeze rustling the tall grass—fuse with their images. A train whistle signals a departure from one mental space and time to another, as the camera hurtles through the bedroom like a locomotive, transporting us to France, where a pale blue sky is punctuated by tall red chimneys and church bells chime. Lucier's camera floats past myriad details—rusted finials on iron gates; blurred, half-glimpsed figures walking amid poplars—gradually giving way to motifs favored by Claude Monet: poppies waving in a field, water lilies blooming in Giverny's pond, and yet another antique room transformed by light filtered through a prism.

The camera moves gently in and out of focus, momentarily dazzled by the images that lie beneath the surface of ordinary reality. All movement becomes emblematic of the mind's faltering, nostalgic journey to discover the beginning and the end of experience. Lucier finally arrives at a blinding white light and a cemetery lane where decaying flowers flutter about a tombstone. A soft light glints upon the surface of a bronze plaque: "A mon oncle." The plaintive whistle of a train converges time, space, and memory in this joyful elegy.

Lucier's personal journey is also a mythic one; it is a search for meaning and kinship, human as well as artistic. As it celebrates innocent discovery, the tape creates a nonverbal, even preliterate,

experience that is bound to plunge the sensitive viewer into a bittersweet meditation on life, death, and collective memory.

Lucier has worked in video, photography, lasers, mixed media, and performance art since the early Seventies. She prefers designing sculptural, multimonitor video installations designed for museums and public spaces. Among her better known multichannel works are *Dawn Burn* (1975–76), *Equinox* (1979), *Denman's Col (Geometry)* (1981), and *Wintergarden* (1984).

One Way

by James Byrne

1979. 8 min. b/w.
Distributor: MOMA. Formats: ¾", VHS, Beta.

In ONE WAY, video artist James Byrne uses his camera as a tool of tactile exploration. Byrne began working in video in 1972, concerned with how video transforms what we see. His tapes often reveal barely discernible fluctuations, like a pulse or deep breathing, a fascination influenced by the perceptual experiments of video artist Peter Campus, who was Byrne's teacher. In ONE WAY, the camera is more dramatic and aggressive, skimming, gliding, floating in space until it crashes into a surface, emphatically, bodily, there. This first-person

viewpoint takes us metallically strumming through a chain-link fence, prowling up a pole, and scraping peeling paint off iron. The sounds of contact are amplified by the camera microphone, which transforms mundane collisions into cataclysmic events.

Byrne carries the camera as though it were an extension of himself, not an expensive piece of equipment. Constantly shifting about, it seems to be free of the law of gravity, and the viewer's sense of ground becomes so disoriented that she, too, begins to feel weightless. Increasingly identified with the camera's perspective, we drag along the pavement and comically bang into a "One Way" sign like a drunk or a madman—or an artist whose dancelike camera gestures liberate us from the normal, boring, and expected world. As Byrne constantly shifts his camera, leaning now left, now right, even upside down, he frames reality in new ways, affording unusual perspectives that draw us into his playful space.

"Paper Tiger Television"
Herb Schiller Reads the *New York Times*—712
Pages of Waste: *The Sunday Times*

by Paper Tiger Collective

1981. 28 min. b/w & color.
Distributors: Paper Tiger Television, Video Data Bank. Formats: ¾",
VHS, Beta.

Credits: Paper Tiger Collective (1981): Diana Agosta, Pennee Bender,
Mary Feaster, DeeDee Halleck, Marty Lucas, Richard Linette, Daniel
Brooks, Skip Blumberg, Valerie Van Isler. *Cameras* Skip Blumberg,
Diana Agosta *Audio* Marty Lucas *Switcher* Pennee Bender *Gloves*
Mary Feaster *Floor Manager* Daniel Brooks *2d camera* David
Schulman *Music* "Don't Lie to Me" *Set* Ron Kelly *Help* Media Bus,
Downtown Community TV Center, Karen Paulsen, Daniel Del Solar.

"Paper Tiger Television" tackles the communications industry much
as David tackled Goliath: With public access cable as the sling and
outspoken media critics furnishing the ammunition, this weekly cable
access show routinely topples the giants of the information industry.
The live, public access program was an outgrowth of "Communications Update," a cable show begun by New York independent
producers DeeDee Halleck and Liza Bear. Herbert Schiller, outspoken
critic and the author of *The Mind Managers* and *Who Knows: Information in the Age of the Fortune 500,* helped Halleck launch this
new series in 1981 with his six-part, razor-sharp analysis of the *New
York Times.* By doing so, Schiller established the series' inimitable
style and its high standards for witty, incisive media analysis in-
formed by knowledge of the media's corporate structures. Schiller's
third and, arguably, best program—712 PAGES OF WASTE: THE SUNDAY
TIMES—epitomizes the provocative content and style of "Paper Tiger
Television."
   With his mordant humor, deadpan expression, and machine-gun
delivery, Schiller dazzles his viewers. In 712 PAGES OF WASTE: THE
SUNDAY TIMES, he leafs through the four-pound paper, pointing up the
missing political context for seemingly neutral articles and drawing
our attention to the relationship (and frequent confusion) between
ads and editorials. After summarily dismissing the Travel Section as
"consumerist fantasies" and the Real Estate Section as "testimonials
to developers—financial con men gouging the system," he briefly
lingers over the Book Review, which publishes reviews of roughly
1,000 of the 50,000 books annually published, and notes the unfair
legitimacy given employment agencies—"prime degraders of the human spirit"—by the want ads. He concludes his illuminating, often
devastating critique by reasserting his claim that the *Times* is the
steering mechanism of America's ruling class.

Even the lively and entertaining Schiller risks becoming a deadly talking head during a half-hour monologue, so inserts of clever "anticommercials"—independent film or video clips—and ironic musical numbers provide visual variety and a change of pace that underscore the issues under discussion. Schiller's backdrop is a mock version of a subway newspaper stand: A cardboard cartoon bearing little resemblance to the slick studio sets used for TV programs, it's more like the set for a third grader's class play. The homemade environment reminds viewers that Paper Tiger's homely, low-tech effort at making alternative TV is intentional, a forceful statement that good television need not be as costly or slick as the networks would have us believe. It's imagination and a rigorous view of the media—not money—that make television memorable and thought-provoking. "Paper Tiger TV" makes a virtue of its limitations, boastfully announcing its budget—$75 to $250 per show for studio rental, title cards, and Magic Markers—in the hand-written credits at the close of each show. Labor is donated by the ever-changing collective of young media makers who pull off each week's show.

Since Schiller's acclaimed premier series, "Paper Tiger TV" has produced more than 80 programs that cover not only American but foreign journals and television systems. Topics have strayed from the original focus on American print publications to such media-related issues as the AT&T breakup, American TV coverage of mass demonstrations, and high-tech snooping. Programs on Nicaragua's press and TV news, on such Soviet publications as *Pravda* and *Sovetsky Sport,* and on Grenadan television have expanded coverage to foreign media. The more popular and successful early programs include psychologist Joel Kovel reading *Psychology Today,* New York intellectual Joan Braderman examining *The National Enquirer,* feminist critic Ynestra King reading *Seventeen,* anarchist philosopher Murray Bookchin on *Time,* and university professor Brian Winston reading *TV Guide.*

Critics have lavished praise on "Paper Tiger Television," hailing it for raising the question of what *could* be presented on commercial television while simultaneously indicating why it is not (Amos Vogel, *Film Comment*), comparing it to Brecht's Didactic Theater (Martha Gever, *Afterimage*), and marveling at how its "cogent and at times offhand analyses of American magazines reveal both the concentrated power and wealth of the print media industry and the impoverished character of the information it disseminates" (Alexander Wilson, *FUSE*). The series has been so well received that it is currently being syndicated to several cable systems around the country. (A VHS special, which includes a half-hour sampler of 20 "Paper Tiger TV" shows plus one complete program selected by the buyer from the catalog, is also available, priced low to accommodate the budgets of home video viewers.)

Perfect Leader

by Max Almy

1983. 4 min. color.
Distributors: EAI, Kitchen. Formats: ¾″, VHS, Beta.

Credits: *Editor* Bud Ryerson *Original Music* Gregory Jones, Roy Sablosky *Lyrics* Max Almy *Computer Graphics* Claire Doyle *Project Consultant* Christine Robbins *Actor* Craig Hammond *Female Voice* Cullyn Anderson *Production Assistants* Dan Belmour, Jon Carradies, Paula Rahn *Music Recording* T & B Audio Labs *Audio Engineer* Gregory Jones. *Thanks* Leo Knapp, Linn Drum Programming. Postproduced at One Pass. *Funding* National Endowment for the Arts.

PERFECT LEADER is a social satire music video. In it, video artist Max Almy creates a biting parody of the political spot, an Orwellian scenario in which an omnipotent computer creates the Perfect Leader. A disembodied Big Brother narrator calls up a menu at this computerized casting session, looking for the prototype: a well-groomed Kennedy clone, played by comedy writer Craig Hammond. It has potential, he says, but needs more charisma. Pleased with the next model, a brown-shirted, wild-eyed Hitler look-alike, this voice-of-God computer programmer wants it stronger and more dominant, but then

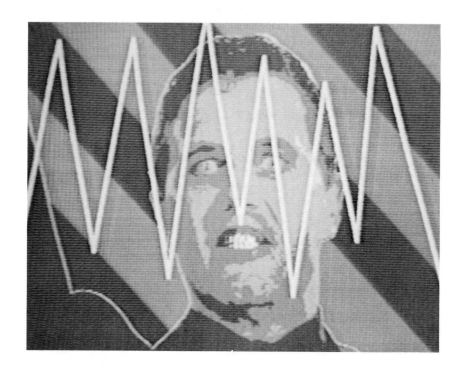

rejects it because "that didn't work last time." "What we need is a little more morality," he says. "That's always been popular." Up pops the earnest posturing of a Bible thumper. (Hammond's miming of all three figures is flawless.)

After configuring the psychological modifications and media impact of marketing projections—the multinational profit factors and global leadership strategies—the computer screen reads out the data, a telling series of icons: dollar bills, cars, TV sets, flags, bombers, guns, and explosions.

Almy's pulsing computer graphics turn the final modulation scene into a cross between a video game and a flight simulation, a hypnotic flicker of alternating images that evokes the diabolical metamorphosis in a sci-fi or horror film. A giant bull's-eye is superimposed over all three prototypes, leading up to a climax timed to the frantic beat of the insistent, insidious pop lyrics "We've got to have the Perfect Leader! We've got to *find* the Perfect Leader!"—a knee-jerking, toe-tapping fascist chant that sends chills down your spine. The final test, of course, is taking the Perfect Leader and framing him on a TV set, the last image frozen on the screen.

Max Almy is a San Francisco–based artist whose computer video tapes have been shown in museums and broadcast on public and cable television. She began working in video in the mid-Seventies and has produced performance and installation pieces in addition to her better-known tapes, *Modern Times, Leaving the Twentieth Century,* DEADLINE, and PERFECT LEADER.

Piano Players Rarely Ever Play Together

by Stevenson J. Palfi

1983. 59 min. color.
Distributors: Stevenson Productions Inc., MOMA. Formats: ¾″, VHS, Beta.

Credits: *Produced/Directed/Written/Edited* Stevenson J. Palfi *Videographers* Arnold Bourgeois, Jim Moriarty *Associate Producers* Arnold Bourgeois, Polly Waring Palfi, Eddie Kurtz *Audio* Eddie Bunkley, Terry Goins *Audio Mix* Steve Darsey *Editor* Stevenson J. Palfi *Camera Director/Music Shooting* David Atwood. Produced in association with Mississippi Educational Television. *Funding* Rockefeller Foundation, Louisiana State Art Council, Alabama Filmmakers Co-Op, National Endowment for the Arts Regional Media Grant, National Black Programming Consortium, Corporation for Public Broadcasting.

As the title says, piano players rarely ever play together. But New Orleans videomaker Stevenson Palfi had the idea of bringing together in concert three great blues musicians: Isidore "Tuts" Washington, one of New Orleans's most gifted musicians, a blues and honky-tonk pianist who was the idol of many young players in the Thirties and Forties; Henry "Professor Longhair" Byrd, the blues, barrel-house, and r&b master affectionately called "The Bach of Rock 'n' Roll"; and Allen Toussaint, well-known songwriter ("Java") and one of the most successful synthesizers and popularizers of New Orleans music.

The tape covers the rehearsals for the concert, affording intimate glimpses of each of the men separately and working together. As they muse over their lives and careers, their rambling, stream-of-consciousness recollections play off the sheer professionalism and exuberance of their very different musical styles. Although the tape sets out to examine three musical generations, its real focus is on Professor Longhair—Fess to his friends. His unique syncopated playing mixed the blues with rumba and samba rhythms. His supersonic triplets in the right hand superimposed over an 8/8 rumba beat in the bass made the blues rock and roll, a style that would later influence Fats Domino, James Booker, and Dr. John, as well as Allen Toussaint. Professor Longhair—a name that summons visions of piano players plying their trade in the bordellos of New Orleans's red-light district, Storyville—was responsible for the unofficial anthem "Mardi Gras in New Orleans," yet despite his versatility and talent, lack of money and recognition plagued him all his life. This concert was to be a showcase of his contributions, and those of Washington, to the

musical heritage of New Orleans. But fate stepped in, and two days before the concert, Fess died. Invited by his widow to tape the jazz funeral, Palfi covered the sorrowful occasion and went on to tape the memorial concert given for him by Tuts Washington and Allen Toussaint.

What we have then is a remarkable rehearsal, where we see and hear the anarchy of three talented soloists crafted into a joint performance under Professor Longhair's surprising direction. Allen Toussaint, too much in awe of his heroes, could not direct the performance, so Fess stepped in, musically sure, and forcefully created a harmony of styles and personalities that bore out Palfi's belief that such a concert would make musical history. PIANO PLAYERS becomes a tape about the creative spirit and its endurance, about collaboration and its pitfalls, and about three lives deeply wedded to the piano and its music. Not only is it a tribute to these performers but also to producer Palfi, who did not let death daunt him in making his tribute.

Palfi, whose background in video was acquired at the New Orleans Video Access Center (NOVAC), where he served as director for several years, started out by making documentaries for the low-income black community of New Orleans. Naturally interested in the music around him, he made his first musical portrait, THIS CAT CAN PLAY ANYTHING, with several other NOVAC staffers. PIANO PLAYERS RARELY EVER PLAY TOGETHER is his most polished, heartfelt work to date. The tape has been broadcast nationally on public television, shown on CBS Cable, and aired in England on Channel Four.

Pick Up Your Feet: The Double Dutch Show

by Skip Blumberg

1981. 29 min. color.
Distributors: EAI, MOMA. Formats: ¾″, VHS, Beta.

Credits: *Producer/Camera/Editor* Skip Blumberg *Audio/VTR* Jan Kroeze, Esti Galili Marpet, Jerry Ross, Richard Young *Additional Camera* Joel Gold, Bill Marpet *Editing Assistant* Carl Bartee *Production Manager* Leanne Mella *Lighting* Jan Kroeze *Production Assistants* Carl Bartee, Wendy Levine, Sharron Robertson, Yvette Spellman. *Thanks* Jane Aaron, The American Double Dutch League, Gwen Maristani, David Walker, Mike Williams, 32nd Precinct Community Council, Brownsville Recreation Center, Educational Alliance, J.H.S. 43, P.S. 1 (Manhattan), St. James School, Technisphere Inc. Produced in association with the Television Lab at WNET/13: *Executive Producer* Carol Brandenburg *Videotape Editor* Scott Doniger *Associate Director* Terry Benson *Post-production Coordinator* Barbara Ravis. *Funding* New York State Council on the Arts, National Endowment for the Arts.

Awards: Emmy; Blue Ribbon, American Film Festival; Video Prize, Global Village Video and Television Documentary Festival.

PICK UP YOUR FEET is a scintillating look into the world of competitive double-dutch jump rope. It opens with several girls jumping to the familiar rhyme "Strawberry Shortcake," then quickly cuts to the far more complicated feats of competitive double-dutch. In a matter of seconds, even the most blasé viewer is as breathless as the contestants, unexpectedly thrilled by the sheer energy and physical skill on display.

The tape chronicles the Eighth Annual World Invitational Double Dutch Jump Rope Championship, held in New York City, and it focuses on four of the most popular teams in the event: the Fantastic Four, the DD Tigers, the Jumping Joints, and the Dynamos. Intercut with sequences from the championship meet are background interviews with coaches and team members and a behind- the-scenes view of practice sessions.

Blumberg lets the girls speak for themselves, communicating their enthusiasm, determination, and nervousness in a way that is strikingly direct and unself-conscious. One turner's driving refrain to her jumper, "Pick up your feet!"—half encouragement, half command—expresses far better than any didactic narrator the merits of team effort and pushing past limits. The girls demonstrate their exacting sport in gyms, playgrounds, and on the Lincoln Center outdoor stage, explaining compulsory speed jumping—five steps per second during a two-minute sprint—and freestyle tricks for singles and doubles—an elaborate choreography of acrobatics, dance steps, handing over the

rope in midjump, turning while jumping, and whatever else the girls are imaginative enough to devise and daring enough to risk.

PICK UP YOUR FEET is a tape about love, sweat, and tears—shed over victory as well as defeat. Its overwhelmingly upbeat impact is a result not only of the remarkable young jumpers but of Blumberg's unique documentary style.

One of the original Videofreex, Blumberg began making tapes in 1968, collaborating with a number of video groups, working as a camera operator and engineer for a public television station, and then launching his own career as an independent producer. His dual life as a video guerrilla and TV engineer led him to a hybrid style that blends the best of television with informal street video. His mix of TV entertainment and documentary information is a far cry from television's exploitive treatment of real people for cheap thrills and sexual innuendo. Blumberg works with people he genuinely respects, and that positive feeling comes across. Another key to his intimate style is his insistence on being both cameraman and interviewer. This means his subject is always talking directly to the camera and, so, to the audience. Add to this his unaffected curiosity and an uncanny knack of asking just the right questions, and you have richly informative, relaxed interviews.

Like the jumpers, Blumberg knows how to push the limits of the medium, using extreme shooting angles and close sound, picking up the pace through montage, and using live-TV editing techniques to make it seem as though the tape is live. With visually stunning camera work, virtuoso editing and pacing, and an irresistible subject, PICK UP YOUR FEET is a breakthrough in the tradition of documentary makers who tried, as Ralph Steiner has said, "to make the terribleness of the world more pleasant."

The Police Tapes

by Alan Raymond and Susan Raymond

1976. 90 min. b/w.
Distributors: Video Verite, Kitchen. Formats: ¾″, VHS.

Credits: *Produced/Videotaped/Edited* Alan Raymond, Susan Raymond. Produced in association with the Television Lab at WNET/13.

Awards: DuPont-Columbia Journalism Award; George Foster Peabody Award; local and national Emmys for Best Documentary.

THE POLICE TAPES is a chilling view of ghetto crime as seen by the policemen of the 44th precinct in the South Bronx, better known as Fort Apache. The tape is structured around the nightly patrols, focusing on ten real-life dramas and the leadership of an above-average commanding officer. Episodes include a street gang spoiling for a fight; an argument between neighbors that has its amusing side; a bloody murder in a social club; a deranged man holding his family prisoner in their apartment; a rape; a welfare story of bureaucratic snafus; a car thief suddenly violent during his arrest; an elderly woman in jail for whacking her daughter with an ax; a conflict between two families over borrowed goods (with a *West Side Story* romantic twist); and an investigation of a brutal knifing.

Interspersed with these real-life dramas is a fascinating interview with Commander Anthony Bouza, who offers a sophisticated analysis of the complex social and political issues underpinning ghetto crime. Explaining cop psychology and his own frustration "at commanding an army of occupation in the ghetto," Bouza concludes:

> We have a subculture in our society and it resides in the ghetto. And we are conditioning this subculture to fail, to become alcoholics, to be violent. And we have given them no other mechanisms

with which to cope. The fact of the matter is that we are manufac-
turing criminals and brutality. We are very efficiently creating a
very volatile and dangerous subelement of our society. And we are
doing it simply because we don't want to face the burdens and the
problems and the responsibilities that their existence imposes on
any society with conscience. . . . To the degree that I succeed, to
that degree I'm deflecting America's attention from this problem.
Maybe I'd be better off failing.

The Raymonds used a low-light video camera to make a documentary that is dramatic, dark, and menacing to watch. Portable
video's nighttime black-and-white images are far more disturbing than
the "living color" of TV crime shows; they are at once more real and
more abstract, so that violence lingers in the mind like a recurrent
nightmare. The Raymonds follow the officers before, during, and
often after each case, revealing much about the men and their percep-
tions of themselves, their roles, and the community they serve. To the
extent that the Raymonds view the ghetto only from these outsiders'
perspectives, never turning the tables to see how the residents view
the cops, it offers a subjective but powerful view of ghetto life and
crime. The dominant view becomes that of the articulate, anguished
Bouza, who offers the final cogent words on cops and ghetto crime.

Well known for their role in the controversial public television
series "An American Family," the Raymonds approached the tape
from their cinema vérité background, avoiding any voice-over narra-

tion, shooting you-are-there footage that is intensely immediate in the vivid video medium. Resembling filmmaker Frederick Wiseman in their shared interest in the larger social and institutional context that shapes human lives, the Raymonds are more pragmatic in their vérité style—shuttling back and forth in time to cover the beginning and end of episodes.

Two years before THE POLICE TAPES, two producers at University Community Video in Minneapolis made *Officers of the Law* for local public television; it is a startling prototype for the Raymonds' work, different only in that it was made in an urban ghetto perhaps less squalid and dramatic than America's highest-crime-rate ghetto but equally torn by racial and economic inequities. Both tapes were driven as much by the emerging video technology, which could make such unobtrusive nighttime shooting possible, as by the Zeitgeist. Ironically, Commander Bouza, who was forced out of his job after THE POLICE TAPES was aired, is now chief of police in Minneapolis.

Distilled from over 40 hours of videotapes, THE POLICE TAPES was produced at the Television Lab at WNET/13. Given both the popular and critical acclaim that met its New York broadcast, a re-edited and streamlined version—50 minutes, which cut out much of the violence and street language—was broadcast in 1978 as an ABC "News Closeup," the first such independent video documentary to be aired on national network TV. Critics vied in their raves: "[It] provides a valuable perspective on the states of both video technology and television journalism. It is by turns shocking, infuriating, disgusting, and surprisingly enough, absurdly funny" (John J. O'Connor, *New York Times*); "*The Police Tapes* needs to be seen by just about everyone. . . . [They] have broken into a territory of an overwhelmingly clear importance, with a message so forceful it doesn't even need to be forced, and that justifies voyeurism like a scream from a neighbor's apartment" (David Elliot, *Chicago Sun-Times*); "A social documentary of the first urgency" (Tom Shales, *Washington Post*).

The low-light lowlife shown to the American public in THE POLICE TAPES has since become weekly dramatic fare in the award-winning TV series "Hill Street Blues," which was modeled on this documentary, as well as nightly fare on the "action news" segments that heat up television. Since 1977, the Raymonds have produced *Bad Boys,* a controversial two-part video study of juvenile crime, and a series of filmed documentaries for ABC, including *To Die for Ireland, The Third Coast,* and *Hooray for Hollywood.* In 1983, they filmed the Loud family again for *American Family Revisited.*

Possibly in Michigan

by Cecelia Condit

1983. 12 min. color.
Distributor: EAI. Formats: ¾″, VHS, Beta.

Credits: *Writer/Director* Cecelia Condit *Score/Music Performance* Karen Skladany *Cast:* Sharon—Jill Sands, Janice—Karen Skladany, Prince Charming—Bill Blume *Explosion Footage* Amy Krick *Photographers at Dance* Amy Krick, Jeff Chiplis *Sound Mixing* David Narosny, Joel Solloway *Final Production Editing* David Narosny *Special Effects* John Barak, Industrial Video Inc. *Thanks* Elizabeth Breckenridge, Jo Caress, Marian Condit, Gloria Deitcher, Carter Dodge, George Farago, MaryAnn Fargo, Jane Farver, Mary Gandee, Ilse Gonzalez, Tim Gooden, Pamela Grosscup, Earl Keys, Bill Kimbel, Meg Kratz, Amy Krick, Mary Lucier, Susie Nabstedt, Tracy Nabstedt, Robert Palmer, Glen Ray, Judith Salomon, Mike Scott, David Simmerer, Stephen Vogel, John Waylko, Joe Whalen, The Cleveland Institute of Art, Group W Cable of North Ridgeville, Ohio. *Funding* National Endowment for the Arts, Ohio Arts Council.

POSSIBLY IN MICHIGAN is a new wave retelling of several Old World fairy tales. In this thinking-woman's music video, Cecelia Condit and composer Karen Skladany explore violence and sexuality against the surreal backdrop of suburban shopping malls and tree- lined, middle-class neighborhoods. Skladany's lilting music box airs alternating with a driving tom tom beat suggest a dialogue between masculine and feminine. Her lyrics narrate this tale because Condit's characters exist in what is part silent movie, part dream state, where images recur with eerie consequences. Condit's characters are archetypes: She collapses Prince Charming, the Frog Prince, and the Wolf into one anthropomorphic prince. Sharon, a dazed innocent whose trancelike behavior evokes Sleeping Beauty, is accompanied by Janice, a female version of the hero's loyal friend. This new wrinkle in heroic conventions is the first in a series of unexpected twists.

Skladany opens by singing: "I bite at the hand that feeds me," suggesting a connection between voracious appetites—for food and sex—and the dependence of women on men. Men feed women only to devour them, a thesis illustrated by men who wear pig heads, reinforcing their cannibalistic, animalistic traits. When Prince Charming tells Sharon, "I will eat you or cut off your arms or legs," and throws her down on the bed, she replies with wistful irony, "Love shouldn't cost an arm or a leg." Janice comes to her aid with a macabre, though fitting, solution. In this modern-day fairy tale, it is Red Riding Hood who devours the Wolf, neatly disposing of his bones in a black plastic trash bag that is completely devoured by a garbage truck.

Condit's imagination is inspired by weird real-life experiences, manipulated to create a contemporary story rich with complex meanings. Her work draws upon the tradition of surreal art, such as the films of Jean Cocteau, as well as today's popular culture, from shopping malls to MTV. With Skladany, Condit reinvents television's soap opera as feminist opera, subverting the soaps' message of feminine submission to male power by substituting an absurdist alternative. Playing off of melodrama, horror-story conventions, and fairy tales, Condit presents a new music statement on the war between the sexes.

Presumed Innocent

by Stefan Moore and Claude Beller

1979. 58 min. b/w.
Distributors: TVG Documentary Arts Projects Inc., MOMA. Format: ³/₄".

Awards: Best Documentary, Emmy Award; Best Documentary, Corporation for Public Broadcasting; Best Documentary, Atlanta Video and Film Festival; Best Documentary, Athens Video Festival.

Taped at New York City's House of Detention for Men on Riker's Island, PRESUMED INNOCENT exposes the plight of men accused of crimes and unable to raise bail. With bail set at anywhere from $500 to $50,000, men without money are detained from three months to two years before even coming to trial. "The system is designed so that they can just keep a person here as long as they feel he belongs here, not as long as he deserves to be here," explains Peter Tufo, chairman of the city's board of corrections. "Where's the equality of the law for us?" one inmate asks, noting that almost 90% of the men are indigent blacks and Hispanics. Suicide, violence, and despair hound the men, packed tightly in filthy cell blocks where anyone can snap at any time. Interviews with prison guards, legal aid lawyers, judges, prison doctors, the director of the Prison Reform Task Force, as well as prisoners and their families paint a sad and sordid view of the criminal justice system.

Judge Bruce Wright, whose lenient bail rulings have won him the ire of New York's mayor, persuasively argues that this system of pretrial detention fails to honor the "presumption of innocence" on which the criminal justice system is based. This award-winning tape is an eye-opening view of how the poor are punished before they are even tried.

Stefan Moore has been a documentary producer since 1968. In 1971, he worked with John Reilly on THE IRISH TAPES, and in 1972, he formed TVG Productions with Claude Beller. It took them a year and a half of negotiating before they were even permitted into the jail and then another year and a half to shoot and edit before the tape could be aired on public television. They have produced a number of film and video documentaries, including *Trouble on Fashion Avenue,* a filmed investigation of sweatshops in New York City's $16 billion-a-year fashion industry, and the *March against Racism,* a tape about the busing conflict in Boston.

The Pursuit of Happiness

by Julie Gustafson and John Reilly

1983. 60 min. color.
Distributor: Global Village. Format: ¾".

Credits: *Producers/Directors* Julie Gustafson and John Reilly *2d Camera* Hart Perry *Sound* Martin Lucas *Additional Sound* Victor Sanchez, Nicole Fauteux. Opening clip of Molly Rush from Emile D'Antonio's *In the King of Prussia. Montage Design* Nathaniel Merril.

THE PURSUIT OF HAPPINESS is the most complex documentary video narrative to emerge in the Eighties. Julie Gustafson parallels the lives of seven individuals who share a common link: prison. It's not just an actual prison but a metaphoric one, one that locks them into mental restraints as chafing as iron chains. By examining what "the pursuit of happiness" means to each person, Gustafson poses hard, thought-provoking questions about the value of human life. Featured here are Ida May and George Petsock, a marvelous couple whose resemblance to Edith and Archie Bunker is funny but misleading, because they are far more complex and human than that comedy series duo. George is the superintendent of the Pennsylvania State Prison; Ida May has followed him to his current job, leaving her roots behind. She longs for a future that her husband George, ever cautious, fears to count on.

At the prison, we meet two lifers: Ron, a Vietnam vet implicated in an armed robbery, hesitantly conducts a romance by mail, afraid to hope he will have any future with his would-be bride outside prison. Walter, a worldly black inmate, knows that for him happiness inside or outside those walls is about the same. Briefly interned in the prison is Molly Rush, a Catholic peace activist whose antinuclear protest with the Ploughshares 8 jeopardized not only her own future but that of her family, especially her husband, Bill. But the way she looks at it, she and all humanity may have no future unless people stand up against the threat of nuclear holocaust. Bill, confused and agonized by his wife's flinty zeal, worries more about the survival of

his marriage than that of the human race, while trying valiantly to understand and support Molly. All the players in this moving human drama are driven by their visions of a meaningful life, one that involves not only their own happiness but that of others.

Gustafson sensitively observes each couple, capturing amazing revelations of character in natural dialogue that surpasses the best writing of talented dramatists. In a passage that rivals Beckett, Ida May and George discuss their retirement and the pros and cons of "planning for" versus "counting on" the future. But since these are not abstract, fictional characters, their unique reality gives added power to the human hopes and fears they face. While editing the tape, Gustafson and her coproducer-husband, John Reilly, thought of the tape as a novel, recognizing literary precedents in constructing their documentary narrative. This is by no means docu-drama, because its reality is unrehearsed and immediate, but it shares with drama a multifaceted artistic shape where characters emerge—complete with tragic flaws—to engage in a story larger than any of them grasp. The tape is a major documentary and artistic achievement, the culmination of Gustafson's documentary career.

Gustafson's tapes have always emerged from personal concerns. Her first work, *The Politics of Intimacy,* was an outspoken discussion of sexuality by women of various ages and backgrounds, including her mother and sister; a later tape, GIVING BIRTH: FOUR PORTRAITS, outlined options for childbirth after her own frustrating experience during the birth of her son. THE PURSUIT OF HAPPINESS is fundamentally about relationships and growing through change, an appropriate topic for a husband-and-wife team to tackle.

Running with the Bulls

by Bill Marpet and Esti Galili Marpet

1978. 58 min. b/w & color.
Distributor: Video Repertorie. Format: ¾″.

Men come from all over the world each June to run with the bulls in Pamplona, Spain. This tape follows Joe Distler, a Brooklyn schoolteacher, on his annual adventure. Fiesta pageantry, religious processions, bullfights, parades, and tests of strength and endurance fill in the time leading up to the main event. "No one runs to prove his manhood," says Matt, a 24-year veteran runner right out of the pages of a Hemingway novel. "It's for the *alegría*—for the lark. There's a deep mystical power when I'm next to the bulls. . . . They know I am in there, in the herd, moving tranquilly among them."

The camera takes us onto the street in the tense moments before the bulls are loosed. Then it follows, amid the jostling excitement, Joe breaking into step with the pack and Matt unexpectedly gored and rushed to the hospital. In RUNNING WITH THE BULLS, we see the force and allure of male bonding, evident in the all-male drinking sessions, the unembarrassed embraces after a run, and the fearful bravado about women ("Women are as dangerous as the bulls"). The tape makes no sociological commentary, leaving it to the viewer to intuit the meaning of a compulsion to endure this primitive race with death. It ends with producer Bill Marpet in the bull ring, trembling in his boots but gamely waving a cloth before a bull calf. He grins and waves, now a participant as well as observer of this age-old ritual.

Sabda

by Dan Reeves

1984. 15 min. color.
Distributor: EAI. Formats: ¾″, VHS, Beta.

Credits: *Producer/Photographer/Editor* Dan Reeves *Associate Producer/Sound Recordist* Debra Schweitzer *Post-production Assistant* Larry Mishkin *CMX Editor/Digital Video Effects* Richard Feist *Post-production Facility* Matrix Video. *Thanks* Lillian R. Katz, Larry Mishkin, Marcia Dickerson, Marilyn and Bob Schweitzer, 185 Corporation. "Kabir's Song" translated by Swami Chidvilasananda; poetry by Nammalvar translated by A. K. Ramanujan; by Kabir, translated by Linda Hess; by Basavanna, translated by A. K. Ramanujan; by Ramprasad Sen, translated by Leonard Nathan and Clinton Seely. *Funding* John Simon Guggenheim Memorial Foundation, New York State Council on the Arts, Port Washington Public Library.

Inspired by Indian poetry, philosophy, and religion, video artist Dan Reeves set out on his own mystical journey through India. SABDA is his lyrical video poem, a collaboration with some of the great Indian medieval poets. In it Reeves succeeds as few Westerners have in revealing the complex reality that is India.

The tape is a visual rhapsody of exquisite, luminous, slow-motion imagery. Reeves's movement vocabulary ranges from breathless still images of a moon between two trees to wide, sweeping arcs that shift ground and transport the viewer into a mental state where Shakti indeed seems to dance amid the flames. Loosely swinging his camera, Reeves addresses the eye level of a tiny child or soars heavenward, as though flinging his camera into the air. His sensuous camera movements are like the gestures of a dancer. Their subtlety and grace are further enhanced by digital video effects, which grab frames at varying rates, producing an illusory sense of reality: In one poignant scene, a woman beggar stands, solid despite her fragile frame, as the material world streams past, transparent and insubstantial.

Over lyrical phrases of people walking, working, begging, playing, over landscapes alive to the harvest picker or strangely still and remote, Reeves graphically displays the poems of Kabir, Nammalvan, Basavanna, and Ramprasa Sen. He thus enters into a dialogue with poets, a dialogue between eternal India and the heart of a Western visionary.

Visual images of elephants, tigers, leopards, water buffalo, and birds weave through the tape, powerful metaphors for states of being in life and death and the hereafter. Throughout, Reeves questions what is real, what is lasting, what is meaningful. What can a poor man do? SABDA is his answer.

Dan Reeves came to international prominence with his award-winning autobiographical tape, SMOTHERING DREAMS. Eager to separate from his searing memories of the Vietnam war, Reeves's recent tapes, such as *Haiku* and *Amida,* have been more poetic, revealing the profound influence of Eastern philsophy, religion, and art on his work.

Selected Treecuts

by Steina

1981. 6 min. color & b/w.
Distributor: The Vasulkas. Format: ¾".

Awards: Ithaca Video Festival

SELECTED TREECUTS rhythmically alternates between black-and-white images of trees blowing in the wind, a computer memory of those trees rendered as a digital, gray-and-white mosaic, and "real" trees, seen in shimmering color. While drawing relationships between these three levels of visual abstraction, Steina also creates a composition for the ear. With audio modulated by the video signal, an om-like sound reverberates, building in intensity as the various visual images cut in and out and the camera zooms in and out on them. The increasing speed of alternation between scenes and their sounds climaxes and subsides like the dying wind in the sunstroked trees. Mathematically balanced in its formal composition, the tape stirs a metaphysical reverie: Steina's images seem to peel away the surface of the natural world and reveal, in all its nakedness and primal energy, the life force at work.

Born in Iceland, Steina trained as a violinist before marrying Woody Vasulka and embarking on an internationally renowned career as a video artist. She is noted for exploring the aesthetics of "machine vision." Although she frequently collaborates with her husband, Steina uses only her first name when producing individual tapes.

SELECTED TREECUTS was made using the Digital Image Articulator, or Imager, a unique instrument the Vasulkas developed with designer Jeff Schier to explore real-time video and image performance. During the 18 months they spent designing the Imager, Steina produced a tape about its design, construction, and use for the Television Lab at WNET/13. Titled *Cantaloup*—the fruit is used as a model to demonstrate how the system works—this tape offers a fairly

simple introduction to what happens and why. Steina's explanations of pixels (picture elements), slices (or layers) of colors and tone, and the advantages of "grabbing" (storing) images in the computer memory are lucid and amusing. Woody's occasional difficulty in understanding Schier happily takes the edge off the viewer's own confusion. Seeing *Cantaloup* is bound to enhance anyone's appreciation of Woody's ARTIFACTS or Steina's SELECTED TREECUTS.

Shopping Bag Ladies

by Joan Giummo and Elizabeth Sweetnam

1977. 45 min. b/w.
Distributor: Ann St. Productions. Formats: ¾″, VHS, Beta.

Credits: *Producer/Director/Camera* Joan Giummo *Sound* Elizabeth Sweetnam.

This arresting study of five women who live on New York City streets shatters stereotypes about those anonymous ragtag figures. One woman longs to take a bath; another complains her legs hurt from standing 18 hours; all of them shun shelters because of theft, distance, and their own mental confusion. An attractive young black woman

114

speaks confusedly of her family and past job as a nightclub dancer. An older woman explains she has been on the streets since her apartment building was bought to make room for a high-rise; she had lived there 38 years and could not face leaving the neighborhood. But the star here, if such there be, is a whiskey-voiced singer who claims to be Betty Hammer, Patti Page, and Shirley Temple, among others. Overweight from malnutrition, she wears a transparent blouse in summer and bundles up in blankets all winter. At first shy, the robust extrovert recounts her jumbled history as stripper, army doctor, mental patient, and composer/singer, finally admitting she was about ready to give up until the video team came along.

Giummo and Sweetnam look beyond the tatters and blank faces for clues to help us understand these wandering women's lives and feelings, capturing their pathos and humor. Under their gaze, these shopping bag ladies are transformed from derelict ciphers into lost human beings worthy of our compassion and understanding.

Signed, Sealed, and Delivered: Labor Struggle in the Post Office

by Tami Gold, Dan Gordon, and Erik Lewis

1980. 45 min. b/w & color.
Distributor: TAMERICK Productions. Formats: ¾″, VHS, Beta.

Credits: *Producers/Directors/Editors* Tami Gold, Dan Gordon, Erik Lewis.

Awards: Red Ribbon, American Film Festival; First Place, U.S. Film and Video Festival; Global Village Video Festival; San Francisco Video Festival.

The idea for this tape began when Tami Gold's husband, a Jersey City, NJ, postal worker then striking for safer working conditions, was fired in 1978. She picked up her camera to document their right to strike and pursued the subsequent firings and stormy union meetings with collaborators Lewis and Gordon. A scene in a bar after a union victory communicates all the beery charm of working-class television heroes, but this stereotype is quickly dismantled by the producers, who portray the postal workers as articulate, politically savvy people who organize and fight effectively to secure their rights and their lives. The dramatic climax of the tape occurs with the death of Michael McDermott, a mail handler crushed to death at the Jersey City Bulk Mail Facility in 1979. This tragedy testified to the strikers' contention that dangerous, factory-like conditions prevail in the nation's post offices. The producers do not hide their partisan view; they capitalize on it to make a strong, clear case on behalf of the workers for safer working conditions, the right to strike, and more responsive union leadership.

A Simple Case for Torture, Or How Not to Sleep at Night

by Martha Rosler

1983. 62 min. color.
Distributor: Video Data Bank. Format: ¾″.

Credits: *Director/Editor* Martha Rosler *Camera* Dieter Froese *Additional Camera* Martha Rosler.

In A SIMPLE CASE FOR TORTURE, Rosler constructs a frightening analysis of the media's manipulation of information on terrorism and torture. She contends that U.S. government and business are involved in human rights violations around the globe, aided and abetted by the mass media. The tape begins rather mysteriously, as Rosler flips through the pages of *Newsweek,* lingering over ads whose messages eerily anticipate future arguments. Stopping at an opinion piece in defense of torture, she uncovers its heart of darkness. The writer of the piece suggests instances where torture is permissible, such as a mother's right to torture and kill in order to secure the whereabouts of her kidnapped child. Rosler deflates the argument by contrasting the lot of mothers in parallel worlds: She juxtaposes news clippings about the mothers of children who have disappeared in Third World countries with scenes of American mothers strolling in a zoo with their babies safely snuggled against their breasts and verbal accounts of babies tortured to death before their mothers' eyes by Latin American death squads reportedly trained by U.S. advisers.

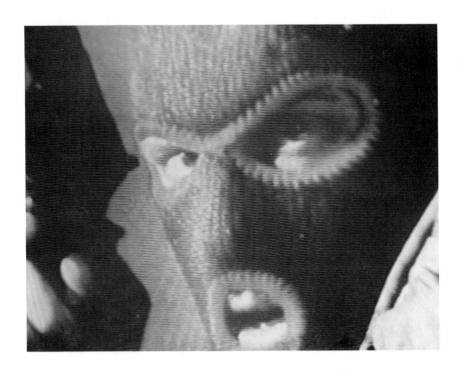

Video may be primarily a medium of the fast-moving image, but in Rosler's hands it becomes a dynamic vehicle for media analysis. She supports her arguments and assertions with writings from accessible sources such as the *New York Times, Time, Newsweek,* and paperbacks found in any university bookstore, giving new meaning to Jean Vigo's definition of documentary: the documented point of view. The tape is dizzying: newspaper clippings, magazine articles, and paperback quotes are rapidly layered over one another, sometimes as texts spoken by voices, sometimes as clippings laid one on top of the other as the camera dances over their surfaces. Rosler's keen logic is relentless, leaving the viewer barely enough time to comprehend the enormity of verbal information and visual associations packed into 60 minutes. If there is a flaw here, it is the driven pace, which practically defies the viewer to keep up with the artist's swift mind and multiple arguments.

Yet because of its density, the tape becomes tremendously involving. Details and evidence mount up, confronting the viewer with the grim possibility that the United States has been guilty of atrocities. Rosler asks us to consider not only whether abuse of human rights has been perpetrated by Americans but the fact that arguments

118

in defense of torture are published with hardly an eyebrow raised. Rosler sets out to raise eyebrows, inviting the viewer to read the media and their messages much more closely.

Smothering Dreams

by Dan Reeves

1981. 23 min. color.
Distributors: EAI, Kitchen, MOMA. Formats: ¾″, VHS, Beta.

Credits: *Producer/Editor/Camera* Dan Reeves *Associate Producer/Production Manager* Debra Schweitzer *Synthesized Music* Jon L. Hilton *Field Engineer* Robert L. Eaton *Studio Engineer/Technical Consultant* Douglas M. Dunning *Additional Camera* Ken Degraff, Philip Mallory Jones, Robert Shea, Phillip Wacker *Sound* Jon L. Hilton, Philip Wilde *Special Effects* Duane Degler, Chris Kuhlthau *Production Assistants* Walter Borton, Bonnie Gordon, Ann Elizabeth Michel, Christy McMillan *Research Assistants* Joseph Friel, Mary Pat Heralko, Ed Ornosky *Soldiers* Michael Page Blowney, Norman S. Easterbrook, Richard (Snooky) Eckert, Hugh Ghiringhelli, Bruce Green, Lenny Haag, Chip Klagstad, Bud Leslie, David Nackman, Phil Oberlander, Jerry Plourde, Darin Shepherd, Lloyd Williams *Nun* Heidi Merrit *Child* Miles Decotiis *Schoolchildren* Michael Abbene, Fred Carpenter, Lorian Dickerson, Barry Dunning, Dawn Dunning, Simeon Furman, Ruth Hardy, Max Ingersoll, John Lewis, Kyle Overstreet, Nicole Roy, Edward Snyder, Chris Stewart, Laurie Weaver. *Thanks* Walter Borton; Challenge Industries; Sue Decotiis; Ken Degraff; ETV Center, Cornell University; Gallagher TV and Electronics; Diane Gayeski; Bonnie Gordon; Bruce Green; Tina Hilton; David and Ellen Ingersoll; Ithaca College; Ithaca Video Projects; Philip Mallory Jones; Ron Kovic; Jim Lauricella; Norma Otero Alvarez; Portable Channel; Marilyn and Bob Schweitzer; Steven Schweitzer; Travlan Films; Trumansburg School District; U.S. Army Film Archives; David Watkins; David Williams; Judy Collins; The Kingsmen; Van Morrison. Produced in association with the Television Lab at WNET/13: *Videotape Editor* Bill Stephan *Associate Director* Al Broderick *Postproduction Coordinator* Barbara Ravis *Executive Producer* Carol Brandenburg. *Funding* New York State Council on the Arts, National Endowment for the Arts.

Awards: Blue Ribbon, American Film Festival; USA Festival.

Dan Reeves was a combat marine trapped in an ambush on the Cua Viet River in January 1969, an event that has haunted him ever since. SMOTHERING DREAMS is his moving autobiographical essay: a cathartic recollection, burning antiwar statement, and searing analysis of the mass media's role in inculcating violence and aggression from childhood onward. The tape borrows its title from the opening line of a poem by Wilfrid Owen:

If in some smothering dreams you too could pace
Behind the wagon that we flung him in,
And watch the white eyes writhing in his face,
His hanging face, like a devil's sick of sin;
If you could hear, at every jolt, the blood
Come gargling from the froth-corrupted lungs,
Obscene as cancer, bitter as the cud
Of vile, incurable sores on innocent tongues—
My friend, you would not tell with such high zest
To children ardent for some desperate glory,
The old lie: Dulce et Decorum Est Pro Patria Mori.

The verse is read over an opening montage of scenes of carnage intercut with little boys playing at war, surreally picking up the helmets of dead soldiers and placing them on their own heads. Weaving together images of his childhood dreams of military glory with adult nightmares of gruesome death, Reeves exposes the fetid reality of combat that those John Wayne movies never hinted at.

In a poetic litany spoken over a collage of old TV shows, movies, archival combat footage, men walking on the moon, and target practice with toy soldiers, Reeves recites: "I was a winner in any gunfight . . . silent, strong, loyal, and shedding not a tear, telling the others to go on and storm the beach. . . . We played it by the book, repeating hand-me-down war stories told by blind men. . . . We were born with television, what better age to learn the lies of war."

Childhood memories of parochial school, where violence was repressed and made all the more menacing, and of military school, where it was harnessed and legitimized, of surreal duck 'n' cover drills and cautionary tales about godless communist atrocities are mingled with glimpses of "the vivid dream." Like a recurrent nightmare, fragments of the ambush appear throughout the tape until the full horror of that helplessness is shown complete at the tape's close. The last scene—a child wandering amid the havoc of bodies lying glassy-eyed in a swamp—is an image of hope as well as a warning.

Some may not be sure where dream ends and memory begins; and it is just this ambiguity that sends viewers back into themselves and memories of "the six o'clock war" and the world that led them there. Transcending the limits of both fiction and documentary, SMOTHERING DREAMS inhabits a terrain that is part familiar, part strange and hellish, where one can experience war stripped of the myths of glory the media fed us.

Trained in film, Reeves's early videotapes shared some of collage filmmaker Bruce Conner's style as well as his preoccupation with violence and apocalyptic destruction. Since SMOTHERING DREAMS, Reeves's award-winning work has fallen more squarely in the realm of video art: He has produced a number of shorter, more lyrical tapes, several either set in India (SABDA) or inspired by Indian religious philosophies (*Amida*).

Some of These Stories Are True

by Peter Adair

1981. 27 min. color.
Distributor: Adair Films. Formats: ¾″, VHS, Beta.

Credits: *Director* Peter Adair *Producers* Gayle Peabody, Pat Jackson *Associate Producer* Judy Epstein *Additional Camera* John Narvaez *Music* "The Drumming, Part IV" by Steve Reich.

Of these three compelling stories on the theme of power, only some of them are true, Adair explains in the opening crawl. In "The Penitentiary," we meet Oscar Tito Perez, a smiling young TV repairman from the South Bronx and a born storyteller. Seated on the plastic-covered sofa in his ornate living room, he relives the morbid prank that put him in solitary and the desperate games he played there to reassure himself that he was still alive. His retelling of his near escape from a would-be rapist exposes his cruelty and smug contempt for "being a woman."

In "West Point," Lucian K. Truscott III recounts his attempt to get mandatory chapel suspended on the grounds that it violated his constitutional rights. His adversary: Regimental Commander Colonel Alexander M. Haig. Truscott, now a writer in New York, is seated in an easy chair in a lamplit, book-lined room. He portrays his challenge to Haig's authority as the courtship of power and control, a struggle imbued with denied sexuality.

In "The Jury," Michael Revson, a nuclear weapons engineer, is found in an airy room with a palm tree. He explains why he held out in a jury case as the question of innocence or guilt disappeared in a personal confrontation between Revson and another juror, their anger building until violence erupted.

These provocative stories link sexual hostility and aggression with the quest for power and raise interesting questions about the nature of truth and reality in documentary. With subtle touches—a plastic-cased sofa, a warm, book-lined study, a chicly minimal room—Adair manages to convey the common themes of male aggression that cut across class, age, and racial barriers. The final image is less subtle in its import: a close- up on a wall photo of a nuclear mushroom cloud. Simply told, these stories and their storytellers are riveting; the revelation that one of them is not true is bound to make viewers either furious for having been taken in or fascinated by the underlying truth in all of them. Equally interesting here is the power of the medium to seduce one into believing that everything that *seems* true *is* true.

Peter Adair, a San Francisco–based documentary producer, is perhaps best known for his feature-length film *Word Is Out*.

The Stag Hotel

by James Morris

1978. 29 min. color.
Distributor: James Morris. Formats: ¾", VHS, Beta.

Credits: *Producer/Director/Editor* James Morris *Camera* Mark Achbar.

Awards: Best Documentary, Athens Video Festival; Ithaca Video Festival; Atlanta Film Festival.

Alcoholism, indigence, and families who do not want them any more mark most of the men living in a decaying center-of-town hotel/bar. Their wives have either left them or died. They are lonely, weak, and without much purpose in life, according to the curiously sympathetic hotel owner. One man, who bears a striking resemblance to George C. Scott, tells how he lost an arm and both feet in work accidents; his tale is bitter and full of both insight and self-deception. Each man is remarkably different, discouraging simple explanations for why they live such a marginal existence. Interviews are mixed with poetic observations–of someone sweeping the floor, another man propped up at the bar and, later, passed out on the floor. Like the squalid cafes painted by a tormented van Gogh, THE STAG HOTEL reveals the haunted reality of some men's lives.

James Morris's style of quiet, powerful observation and elegant, architectural structure invariably focuses on the byways of American culture. He has produced a number of award-winning half-hour documentaries, many for public television. *Journey to the Mountain* traced the comeback attempt of an aging welterweight boxing champ, *Rehearsal* examined what rock 'n' roll music means to lower-income American youth aching to achieve the American Dream, and *Snapshot* explored one of America's pervasive obsessions.

Sunstone

by Ed Emshwiller

1979. 3 min. color.
Distributors: EAI, MOMA. Formats: ¾″, VHS, Beta.

Credits: *Computer Animation* Alvy Ray Smith, Lance Williams, Garland Stern at New York Institute of Technology. *Funding* John Simon Guggenheim Memorial Foundation.

SUNSTONE is a transcendent, three-minute mythic journey by a major pioneer in video art. Emshwiller, who began as a painter and later turned to mixed media and experimental film before discovering video, has been working in the electronic medium since the early Seventies. Using state-of-the-art computer graphics animation at the New York Institute of Technology, Emshwiller worked over a period of eight months to richly explore the three-dimensional possibilities of the video screen in SUNSTONE.

The tape opens with a blank slate from which Emshwiller models a solar disc which is then transformed into the tranquil features of a childlike face: Eyes blink, mouth opens, tongue flutters leaflike and floats until it lodges above the eyes, forming a third eye. Suddenly the part-whimsical, part-mystical image cracks and shatters, radiating intense iridescent light. First the face is reconstituted as a rotating three-dimensional cube, whose other surfaces exhibit still and moving images. Emshwiller zooms in on one, revealing a landscape wherein a man walking becomes a series of men, in a manner reminiscent of Eadweard Muybridge's locomotion studies. Then the original innocent face returns, restored in a thunderclap.

Emshwiller's background as an artist and sci-fi illustrator is delightfully evident in the images he has selected to playfully manipulate. Emshwiller, as godlike creator of an anthropomorphized sun, moves from stone carving to a futuristic three-dimensional movie cube spinning in space and encapsulates the history of art and communication in just under three minutes. The exquisite simplicity and whimsy of the tape belies its significance as a pivotal step in the development of digital computer graphics animation.

TeleTapes

by Peter D'Agostino

1981. 27 min. color.
Distributor: EAI, MOMA. Formats: ¾″, VHS, Beta.

Credits: *Thanks* Deirdre Dowdakin, Brita D'Agostino, Tess Moore, Jed Hanna, David Williamson, Bob Keil, Independent Video, Janice Putney, Electronic Arts Intermix, Wright State University, The Experimental Television Center. *Music* "30's" (Thirties) with Pulse by John Gibson. Produced in association with the Television Lab at WNET/13: *Videotape Editor* Bruce Follmer *Associate Director* Terry Benson *Production Coordinator* Barbara Ravis *Executive Producer* Carol Brandenburg.

In TELETAPES, video artist Peter D'Agostino analyzes television and the way it shapes reality. The tape is divided into three parts: TeleTricks, which examines TV advertising; TeleGames, which explores TV news; and TelePuzzles, which looks at TV movies. Using language, symbols, interviews, and a revealing game for each section, D'Agostino constructs an elaborate analogy to television's own mosaic

A Vast Waste Land

structure, a complex collage examining television as information and entertainment while critically questioning its impact.

The artist's deft critical methods are evident in his motifs: Sleight-of-hand card tricks stand as a metaphor for commercials; a checkers game provides a visual analogy to Nixon's "Checkers" speech; provocative interviews with children about the nature of television reveal their sophistication and naiveté. But D'Agostino's most powerful motif is the recurrent image of a baby in a crib apparently watching a television that is off-screen. Though heard, television is never seen in TELETAPES; it is, in McLuhan's words, the invisible environment D'Agostino strives to render visible and accountable. Is television the baby's pacifier? Who, then, is the baby? When D'Agostino superimposes the words "A Vast Wasteland" on his infant's mattress, the baby becomes a metaphor, and the legend, a disturbing warning.

D'Agostino ends his complex critique on a question: "Telecommunications, is it a right or a privilege?" His fascinating effort to reinterpret television, exposing it as a medium controlling our notions of reality from infancy onward, begs us to consider how that technology should be used and who should have control over it. "If telecommunications were considered a right, the technology would be forced to put itself to the service of the people." As a media artist and critic, D'Agostino's analysis is as timely as it is provocative.

30 Second Spots

by Joan Logue

1982. 15 min. color.
Distributors: EAI, Kitchen. Formats: ¾″, VHS, Beta.

Credits: *Producer* Joan Logue *In collaboration with:* Mary Anne Amarcher, Laurie Anderson, Robert Ashley, David Behrman, John Cage, Lucinda Childs, Douglas Ewart, Simone Forti, Jon Gibson, Philip Glass, Spalding Gray, Joan Jonas, Bill T. Jones, George Lewis, Alvin Lucier, Meredith Monk, Max Neuhaus, Nam June Paik, Charlemagne Palestine, Liz Phillips, Tony Ramos, Steve Reich, Carlos Santos, Richard Teitelbaum, Yoshi Wada, Arnie Zane. Co-produced by The Kitchen: *Producer* Mary MacArthur *Associate Producers* Gregory Miller, Carlota Schoolman *Videography* Joan Logue *Audio* Tom Jung *Lighting* Howard Grossman *Assistant to Producer* Roberta Oese. Produced at Corporate Video Services: *Videotape Editor* John Custodio, Nexus Productions *Editing* Joan Logue *Audio Consultants* George Lewis, Richard Teitelbaum. *Thanks* Sony Corporation of America. *Funding* New York State Council on the Arts, National Endowment for the Arts.

Like a long-playing record of favorite hit tunes or an anniversary sampler of memorable skits from "The Ed Sullivan Show," 30 SECOND SPOTS is Joan Logue's adaptation of a mass market, pop-culture marketing strategy for a rather unlikely purpose: showcasing the work of some of the most prominent figures in American avant-garde music, dance, and video and performance art. Tailored to a television commercial's 30 seconds, Logue's ads for artists concisely present the preoccupations and expressions unique to 25 performers.

Highlights of these signature statements include the ironic, deadpan storytelling of performance artist Spalding Gray and of composer Robert Ashley, speaking a story with his eccentric, singsong intonation, turning it into an unexpected musical experience. When choreographer Bill T. Jones dances with Arnie Zane, a mere push can shatter their images. When intermedia artist Meredith Monk sings, a tight close-up renders her lips poster-sized and her sounds haunting. To accommodate such disparate, individual visions, Logue stretches the limits of video's sound and imagery, but sometimes, all she does is observe. Last to appear is Nam June Paik, video art's Big Dada and a pioneering Fluxus member. He is sitting at a piano with a Styrofoam cup. He hesitates, bends over, and bangs his head on the keyboard. Paik's performance exemplifies what each artist's work delivers, the shock of awareness. Each statement has a curiously bracing effect, compelling viewers to see, hear, and think in new ways. Logue's genius is in being a transparent vehicle to this end.

This Cat Can Play Anything

by Stevenson J. Palfi, Andrew Kolker, and Eddie Kurtz

1977. 29 min. color.
Distributor: New Orleans Video Access Center (NOVAC). Formats: ¾″, VHS, Beta.

Credits: Produced by the New Orleans Video Access Center: *Executive Producer* Stevenson J. Palfi *Camera* Andy Kolker *Interviewer/Sound* Eddie Kurtz. Edited at Synapse Video Center: *Coordinator* Dean Irwin *Engineer/Editor* Tom Klemesrud.

Awards: Best Documentary, Philadelphia International Film Festival; Best TV Documentary, New Orleans Press Club Award; Merit Award, Mississippi Media Festival; Best Documentary, Athens Video Festival; Ithaca Video Festival.

This is an endearing portrait of the legendary black banjo player Emmanuel Sayles. Among his many distinctions, Sayles was in the first racially mixed set in New Orleans, and he has played everything—Dixieland, blues, Latin, jazz—prompting violin virtuoso Papa John Creach to say admiringly in the tape, after a nostalgic set with him, "This cat can play anything!" Music by the Kid Thomas Preservation Hall Band and the Louis Cottrell Band establishes the rich New Orleans musical tradition, and music historian Al Rose explains Sayles's unique place within this heritage. Sayles reminisces with some of his old cronies and finally admits unashamedly he would die of grief if ever he couldn't play his music. The producers communicate their affection for this remarkable septuagenarian and their reverence for a musical past fast disappearing.

THIS CAT CAN PLAY ANYTHING was produced by three members of the New Orleans Video Access Center (NOVAC), founded by VISTA volunteers in the early Seventies to produce programs for New Orleans's low-income, information-poor black community. Best known outside New Orleans for their waiting-room television series "Survival Information Television," NOVAC has produced several award-winning documentaries for local television. THIS CAT CAN PLAY ANYTHING was aired nationally on the PBS "Southbound" series. Palfi went on to produce PIANO PLAYERS RARELY EVER PLAY TOGETHER, and Andrew Kolker teamed up with another NOVACer, Louis Alvarez, to make ENDS OF THE EARTH: PLAQUEMINES PARISH, LA.

Tongues

by Shirley Clarke, in collaboration with Sam Shepard and Joseph Chaikin

1982. 20 min. color.
Distributor: EAI. Formats: ¾″, VHS, Beta.

Credits: *Editors* Shirley Clarke, Steven E. Browne *Music* Sam Shepard *Additional Musical Improvisations* Skip La Plante *Music Performance* Skip La Plante *Camera* Walter Edel, Michel Auder *Executive Producer* Women's Interart Center, Inc. Produced by The Other Theatre *Administration* Performing Artservices *Production Services* Fred Baker Films *Technical Facilities* Vector Video Productions, Inc. *Postproduction Services* Video Transitions, Inc., Hollywood, CA *Video* Nick Besink *Audio* Walter Loehr *Art Director* Christina Weppner *Assistant Art Director* Regan Cook *Original Theatrical Lighting* Beverly Emmons *Lighting Designer* Alan Adelman *Costume Designer* Mary Brecht *Assistant to the Director* Daniel Moran *Production Stage Manager* Ruth Kreshka. Produced in association with the Women's Interart Center: *Executive Producers* Margot Lewitin, Veronica Geist *Production Manager* Byeager Blackwell *Script Supervisor* Colette Brooks *Assistant Recording Engineer* Amy Scarola *Gaffers* Mark Hoxie, Nancy Magline *Wardrobe* Murphy Birdsall *Production Assistants* Dudu Continentino, Corine Scott. *Funding* New York State Council on the Arts, National Endowment for the Arts.

Several years ago, actor-playwright Sam Shepard collaborated with virtuoso actor Joseph Chaikin on two extraordinary one-act plays, *Savage/Love* and *Tongues.* These brief, one-man plays, with their touching, painful revelations about love and death, invite analogies with Samuel Beckett's spare theater. Unlike Shepard's more macho and violent dramas, these are delicate, introspective works, at times funny, poetic, mad, and deeply moving. They provide the prodigiously talented Chaikin with a flexible vehicle for a virtuoso performance. Chaikin is seen at the peak of his performance life in both tapes.

Veteran film and video maker Shirley Clarke collaborated with Chaikin and Shepard in translating their experimental theater to tape. Clarke's own background in dance and theater and her knowledge of video language and space brought some new dimensions to the plays. Each tape commands viewing, although *Savage/Love,* which was staged first for video, was somewhat less successfully translated by Clarke: Her cameras switched between Chaikin and the small troupe of musicians who accompanied him, but what Clarke hoped would preserve the relationship between the rhythms of music and language in the play instead became distracting, a confusion of focus. With TONGUES, Clarke succeeded brilliantly by inventing a variety of imaginative and precise video strategies for recreating the play as

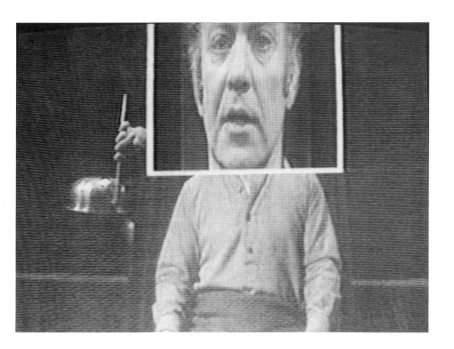

video. The original staging simplified things: A black-robed and -hooded musician plays behind a seated Chaikin. This stillness gave Clarke free range, and she used sophisticated video post-production editing technology with the same fluency, economy, and inspired purpose as Chaikin used his voice and body.

Clarke uses special effects—split screens, feedback, slow- motion, zooms, computer manipulation—to underline the complexity of character states. She blows up Chaikin's face and digitizes it, fragmenting his image into a mosaic of detached particles; she elongates, shrinks, and squeezes his face as his character tries to fit himself into a mold so that people will accept him. Clarke subtly alternates between camera angles during a dialogue, editing tightly to make the most of Chaikin's infinitely subtle shifts of intonation. She jump-cuts to punctuate a revelation, zooms rhythmically to express the ticking clock of time passing in his life. And she slows down his movements, creating an equivalent distortion to the thoughts he is speaking. Without calling undue attention to her techniques, Clarke's video choreography becomes a transparent veil through which we discover the tortured internal monologues and surreal dialogues, the poetic reveries and hallucinatory musings that Chaikin and Shepard have poetically shaped.

Shirley Clarke produced such highly acclaimed films as *The Cool World* and *Portrait of Jason* in the Sixties. In 1971, she discovered video and became a formative figure in the experimental New York video scene. Her daughter, Wendy Clarke, who was a pivotal member of Shirley's video-theater performance group, T.P. Videospace Troupe, went on to establish her own reputation as a video artist with THE LOVE TAPES. Both Clarkes are active video artists today.

Travels

by Shalom Gorewitz

1980. 30 min. color.
Distributors: EAI, Kitchen. Formats: ¾", VHS, Beta.

Credits Includes five works: *Measures of Volatility* (1979. 6 min.); *El Corandero* (1979. 5 min.); *Excavations* (1979. 6 min.); *Autumn Floods* (1979. 6 min.); *Delta Visions* (1980. 5 min.). Image Processing at Experimental Television Center, Owego, NY. Edited with Peter Kirby, Video Transitions, Los Angeles, CA. *Funding* National Endowment for the Arts, New York State Council on the Arts.

Shalom Gorewitz, an acknowledged master of computer-processed video art, creates videotapes that are exquisitely realized moments of intense awareness. In TRAVELS, Gorewitz's journeys across the United States and in Spain and Israel provide the material reality for his poetic explorations, but it is during the long hours of post-production work with the computers, synthesizers, and colorizers at the Experimental TV Laboratory in Owego, NY, that Gorewitz creates his highly subjective visions. In each work, Gorewitz establishes the uniqueness of the moment through color, image, and sound, combining all these elements in a live "performance" at the editing mix. Just as Gorewitz's expression is highly individualistic, the viewer's response is equally so.

Measures of Volatility was shot on a journey across the United States. In it, Gorewitz edits together images of trucks on highways, tract housing, industrial parks, and disembodied, soundless heads, vividly colorizing them to produce an oddly disquieting feeling of impending death, imminent catastrophe, and collapse. By contrast, *El Corandero (The Faith Healer),* shot in Andalusia, Spain, on the artist's wedding trip, is charged with the surreality of a hero's prophetic dream: Trees, roads, weeds, and flowers are all washed with Baudelairean colors. Gradually, the buzzing cacophony of indecipherable village voices ebbs away as flamenco music announces the arrival of a lone dog—like Buñuel's Andalusian Dog—ablaze with red and yellow light in a wide, dusty street. Made in Israel, *Excavations* seems apocalyptic, with its thunder, flickering bolts of lightning, and blood red fields. *Delta Visions,* shot in Florida, is lush with the tropical oranges, golds, greens, and reds that sensuously paint palm trees, flowers, boats, flamingoes, and long-necked birds floating in water. Each Gorewitz tape is a wordless lyric, alive with a poetic

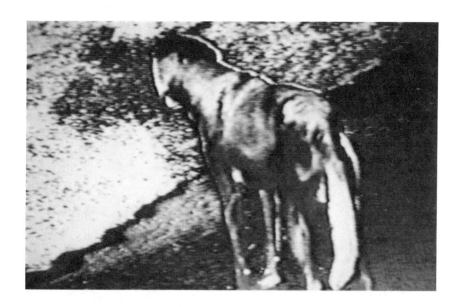

ambiguity that draws upon each viewer's imagination and feelings for interpretation.

The 21st Annual World Eskimo-Indian Olympics

by Skip Blumberg

1983. 27 min. color.
Distributor: EAI. Formats: ¾", VHS, Beta.

Credits: *Producer/Director/Camera/Editor* Skip Blumberg *Audio/VTR/ Lighting* Jan Kroeze *Production Engineer* Dann Farquhar *Videotape Editor* John J. Godfrey *Production* Andy Aaron, Jane Aaron, Sandy Osawa, Margie Schwartz *Photographer* Charles Backus *Assistant Editor* Esti Galili Marpet. *Second Unit: Camera* Ed Guiragos *Audio/VTR* Doug Gedney *Events Announcers* Al Grant, Chris Anderson. *Thanks* Olive Anderson; Daphne Gustafson; Richard Franks; Sarah Scanian; The World Eskimo-Indian Olympics Committee; Roger Kunayak, Sr.; Jim Savok, Jr.; Chuck McConnell; Jeff Fay; KUAC-TV, Fairbanks; Leanne Mella; Rick Kemp; N.W. Arctic School District; Native Trade Fair, Kotzebue, Alaska; Willie Hensley; John Shaeffer; N.A.N.A.; Stephanie Harlan; Susan Subtle; Jules Backus; Hackney/Holden Productions; Barbara Scott; Patty Gymnasium. *Funding* Program Fund of The Corporation for Public Broadcasting.

High spirits and the toss of a blanket send Native American athletes soaring into the air in the exhilirating opening to Skip Blumberg's

delightful tape, THE 21ST ANNUAL WORLD ESKIMO-INDIAN OLYMPICS. High above the Arctic Circle, Olympic athlete Reggie Joul instructs young Eskimos in the games that were once survival training for their ancestors. Joul, who has been competing in the Olympics since 1970, is a major figure at the games and an unofficial spokesperson throughout the tape. Blumberg follows him and Carol Pickett, cutting between the actual events in Fairbanks, Alaska, and Pickett's training to surpass the record for women's high kicks. At 5′3″, the petite and personable Pickett can kick 6′9″ high with one foot. Interviewing her in the modern kitchen where she is preparing a pork chop supper, Blumberg asks Pickett how she became interested in the games. She tells how strangers started calling her racist names. "I am a native, and I want to be proud of it," she says, explaining how the games gave her a means of fighting back.

Blumberg interviews contestants in a seal-skinning race and sure-footed competitors of the greased-pole walk. His camera, close to the ground, follows several men in the grueling endurance test of the knuckle walk. Despite the inevitable atmosphere of competition, camaraderie and good sportsmanship pervade the games. When Pickett unexpectedly breaks all the records, she is mobbed by competitors who embrace her, celebrating her victory as their own. Blumberg's enthusiastic tape reveals how the games are a celebration of the strength of the Eskimo community and its traditions. "We set records, but we haven't come close to breaking the records of our elders," Joul says. "We haven't broken the records of our forefathers." The tape closes with everyone "dancing their hearts out" on the gym floor in joyful expression of their communal strength and pride.

Skip Blumberg's interest in warming up the cool medium of television often leads him to out-of-the-way places and unfamiliar events where people burning calories make television warm and inviting. Best known for his Emmy Award–winning tape PICK UP YOUR FEET: THE DOUBLE DUTCH SHOW, Blumberg has also produced tapes on an elephant round-up in Thailand, a bicycle orchestra, an ugly dog contest, a festival of musical saws, and *The First International Whistling Show.*

Video: The New Wave

by Fred Barzyk for WGBH-Boston

1973. 59 min. color.
Distributor: EAI. Formats: ¾″, VHS, Beta.

Credits: *Writer/Narrator* Brian O'Doherty *Producer/Director* Fred Barzyk *Associate Producer* Olivia Tappan *Researcher* Dorothy Chiesa *Additional Photography* Boyd Estus, Joe Vitigliano, Roger Haydock, Tim Hill *Film Editor* Joan Barkhausen *Videotape Editors* David Crane, David Hutton, Pat Kane, John McKnight, Tom McSorley. *Thanks* National Centre for Experiments in Television; Television Lab at WNET/13; David Ross, Curator of Video Art, Everson Museum; Howard Wise, Electronic Arts Intermix; Leo Castelli Gallery; Sonnabend Gallery; Russell Connor; Sam Mercer; Mary Fenstermacher; Mike McEachern; Chris Noll; Parker River National Wildlife Refuge; The Smithsonian; Adage, Inc.; Bob Lewis; Ed Kammerer *Closing Credits* Based on an idea by Don Rubin. *Funding* National Endowment for the Arts.

VIDEO: THE NEW WAVE is a historic document of the early work of pioneering video artists. Art critic Brian O'Doherty introduces the tape and serves as its host. His discussion of television's vast wasteland is coyly emphasized by the setting, an arid desert with a flickering TV set. Referring to the vast public image bank of televised events—the Ruby-Oswald killing, the Vietnam War, the first men on the moon—O'Doherty notes how the introduction of portable video in the mid-Sixties made possible a new kind of television, one created for smaller audiences by individual artists. This program explores that work, beginning with countercultural tapes, but emphasizing the more publicized work of artists working with abstract feedback images or their own avant-garde scenarios.

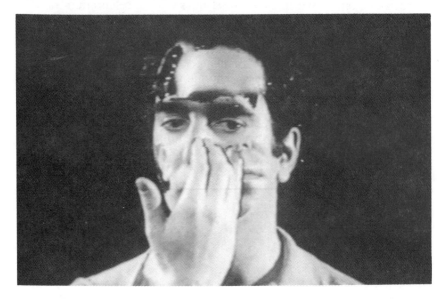

Samples of "guerrilla television" include excerpts from TVTV's FOUR MORE YEARS, produced at the 1972 Republican Nominating Convention, an unprecedented street tape by Angel St. Nuñez interviewing ghetto kids who have just robbed a clothing store, and a clip from Fred Simon's *Bobby The Fife,* a devastating portrait of a young derelict—the sort of story, O'Doherty explains, that "never reaches the TV screen."

Featured next are artists working with feedback: sensuous, ever-changing, infinity images produced by a camera turned on by a live monitor or by a synthesizer. Made by "apostles of technological utopianism and mysticism," such work was either praised for its visual sophistication or reviled as "moving wallpaper." Excerpts from tapes by Doug Davis, Dan Sandin, William Etra, Willard Rosenquist, Bob Lewis, Stan VanderBeek, and Rudi Stern display the seductive magic of whirlpool images timed to musical scores. Artist-engineers working at experimental video labs are also highlighted, including Ron Hays, John Godfrey, Stephen Beck, and Warner Jepson.

For a comical TV collage, Walter Wright taped a grade B Japanese movie off-air, colorizing and keying the images to create an amusing "pychedelic comic strip." James Seawright explored the curious affinity of video and dance, producing an extraordinarily beautiful performance that separated the red, green, and blue components of a three-tube camera to create three ghostly images of one dancer moving in a time-delayed choreography with herself. Donald Hallock presented a "time painting" of photographs of his father. And Nam June Paik, the "George Washington of Video," is represented by several works, including an excerpt from his electronic opera featuring avant-garde cellist Charlotte Moorman and a clip from GLOBAL GROOVE.

Simplicity is the key element in humorous tapes by William Wegman and Eugene Grayson Mattingly. Wegman's sardonic humor is evident in one of his famous skits with his dog Man Ray, "The Spelling Lesson." Mattingly depicts a fantasy flight using the camera as a point-of-view device. Frank Gillette, hailed by O'Doherty as video's most brilliant camera manipulator, offers hypnotic views of a seascape.

Sixties' art conventions are explored and even satirized in several works. Steina plays off of body art with a telephoto close-up of her mouth lip-synching the words to the Beatles' "Let It Be." Inspired by Sixties' happenings, Paul Kos creates a complex environment where the "content is the process"; he switches between two documentary cameras trained either on a block of ice melting over a fire or on a light bulb slowly lowered to the floor and swung in widening circles. And Gerald Byerly's "Process" describes the location of a house by tracing its perimeters with adhesive tape.

Several artists explore the optics of video and the human eye. Joan Jonas is represented by two tapes, one by herself, the other with artist Richard Serra. In the former, she uses a mirror to confound the left-right polarities of the video monitor; in the latter, Serra switches between two cameras trained on Jonas for a fragmented, left brain right brain portrait.

Shown in its entirety, Peter Campus's *Three Transitions* is a real-time video process that also depends on two cameras. Consisting of three movements, it opens with Campus standing with his back to the audience. He cuts a hole in a paper wall and steps through it. But another camera, trained on the other side of the wall, is superimposed on our view so that Campus appears to have passed through himself in an Alice-in-Wonderland visual puzzle. In the second, Campus paints his face with chroma-key blue, which allows him to key, or replace, this image with another one. He effectively erases himself only to reveal another live image of himself within the outlines of his outer mask. In the last, Campus holds a live image of himself on a piece of paper (this is also accomplished with the chroma-key technique). He then sets the paper aflame and watches, noticeably disturbed, as his image burns and disappears. Each of these puzzles exhibits Campus's dry wit, his fascination with video as a surveillance tool, and his penchant for questioning the reliability of perception in measuring reality.

The final tape excerpted is *Scapemates,* by computer video pioneer Ed Emshwiller. Here, dancers move in a surreal landscape, interacting with monolithic, undulating computer images in a sci-fi world of playful abstract manipulations.

VIDEO: THE NEW WAVE fixes a moment in time, revealing standards within the underground video community that were then undergoing change. This extraordinary document is notable for the number of artists mentioned who no longer work in video and for the many who have come to prominence since 1975 whose work was not included in this sampler. It is notable, too, in that an entire category of work—multichannel, sculptural installations, a significant style in early video—was excluded here, no doubt because of the difficulty of translating to a single-channel tape.

Initial enthusiasm for anything made on tape—documentaries as well as abstract and conceptual experiments—by 1975 was giving way to a decided preference for video art, a trend that would become even more pronounced in the Eighties. The original fascination with pure imagery and video feedback, much in evidence here, would fade during the Seventies, replaced by preoccupations with experimental and neoexpressionist narrative, a category unheard of in video's growing years.

VIDEO: THE NEW WAVE chronicles a transitional moment in the history of independent video. Despite its limitations of perspective and taste—or perhaps because of them—it contributes an important chapter on independent video's first decade.

Vietnam: Picking up the Pieces

by Jon Alpert and Keiko Tsuno

1978. 58 min. color.
Distributors: DCTV, EAI. Formats: ¾", VHS, Beta.

Credits: *Producers/Directors* Keiko Tsuno, Jon Alpert *Associate Producer* Karen Ranucci *Editors* John J. Godfrey, Keiko Tsuno, Jon Alpert.

In December 1977, Downtown Community Television Center (DCTV) went to Vietnam, the first American journalists allowed in Vietnam since the U.S. withdrawal in April 1975. This is their frank view of life in Saigon (now Ho Chi Minh City), Hanoi, and the Vietnamese countryside. Jon Alpert introduces the tape and links its episodic structure with a fresh, eyewitness narration that covers black market activity; the Center for the Redignification of Women (which rehabilitates prostitutes); farms, or "new economic zones," reclaiming the defoliated and mined fields; Communist re-education camps; factories; religion under a socialist state; a state-run rehab center for drug addicts; war museums; and more. All but one of the interviews are with ordinary people, the real victims of war: an embittered doctor from Bach Nai Hospital in Hanoi, which was destroyed by a

U.S. air strike that also killed 32 doctors and medical students; a 14-year-old prostitute; a former U.S. translator who is now an opium addict; and some of the 800,000 orphans left in the wake of war. The tape ends in an orphanage, where many children of American servicemen are shown. In what the *Village Voice* conceded was the most moving scene on television in the past ten years, a little Amerasian girl begins to cry, and Alpert asks why she is sad. She replies that he reminds her of her father, who died when she was four. "Everyone is dead," she says simply. "I miss them."

Alpert and Keiko Tsuno show the Vietnamese as valiant in their efforts at rebuilding their war-torn world. By presenting a sympathetic view of the Vietnamese people in the throes of reconstruction, they question what America's responsibility should be to help them.

Aired nationally in July 1978, the program drew strong response. "They let the camera talk," the *Detroit News* wrote. "The viewer slowly begins to see the Vietnamese as human beings and gets a good feeling of the fabric and quality of life in postwar Vietnam. . . . top-notch work that deserves—demands—to be viewed."

Alpert has since returned to Vietnam on behalf of NBC to cover the invasion of Cambodia and the border war with China (*Southeast Asia Report: Cambodia—Vietnam—China*), then on to Iran and Afghanistan (*Reports from Iran and Afghanistan*), and Central America (*The War in Nicaragua; El Salvador: Nowhere to Run*). Rushing in where network crews could not—or would not—go, Alpert has used his Third World contacts and sympathies in reporting on international and domestic trouble spots for American TV audiences. (See also CHINATOWN: IMMIGRANTS IN AMERICA, CUBA: THE PEOPLE, and HEALTHCARE: YOUR MONEY OR YOUR LIFE.)

What's Expected of Me?

by Theresa Mack

1979. 30 min. b/w.
Distributor: Women Make Movies. Format: ¾".

Credits: *Camera/Interviewer/Writer* Theresa Mack *Additional Interviews* Maria Iano, Daniel Mack *Sound* Maria Iano, Daniel Mack, Jim Hollander, Cindy Castleman. Edited at Electronic Arts Intermix: *Editor* Ann Volkes.

Awards First Prize, Sixth Annual Global Village Video and Television Documentary Festival; Fourth Annual Independent Film & Video Festival.

WHAT'S EXPECTED OF ME? probes what one crucial year of growing means in the life of Renee, a bright, articulate, and personable 12-year-old girl living in New York City. The tape opens with a shot of kids playing on seesaws in a schoolyard. It is a significant image because Renee and her sixth-grade classmates are trying to strike a difficult balance between powerful opposing forces in their young lives: conformity versus individualism, adult approval versus peer acceptance.

At 12, Renee is a round-faced tomboy at P.S. 75 on Manhattan's Upper West Side. She enjoys sports, has no "number one" best friend, and is anxious about what will happen to her in junior high. At 13, Renee is in an accelerated academic program at J.H. 104. She has lost weight and changed her blunt-cut hair for a curly, more feminine style. Some of her anxiety has abated: "I know the kids, I know the teachers, I know what's expected of me." But these worries have been replaced by new ones. She is surprised to find herself increasingly at odds with her parents—"I always thought conflicts were for people who had home problems"—and torn by her desire to be accepted by the boys and excel in her academic career. "Sometimes boys resent it that I'm intelligent. Sounds stupid. Why should anyone resent someone being intelligent?"

Theresa Mack works in the celebrated documentary tradition of Robert Flaherty, but she does not venture to exotic locales to find a heroic figure as Flaherty does in *Moana*; Mack looks closer to home, exploring a common though equally heroic rite of adolescent passage. She spends hours with Renee, getting to know her so well that the camera responds intuitively to Renee's thoughts and moods. Tightly cropped close-ups of Renee with her friends suggest the intimacy and exclusivity of such bonds. Moving quickly and smoothly, Mack's

camera anticipates Renee's movements playing ball or walking down the aisle for graduation, pulling back when she is withdrawn and moving in when she is ready to share her thoughts.

Though focused on Renee, the tape features cameo portraits of some familiar teachers—a shrieking choral leader, a pep-talking principal, a harried disciplinarian—that capture the arbitrary, authoritarian, often incomprehensible behavior of adults as viewed by adolescents. Renee's parents disclose their own struggle, trying to exercise some control without being overprotective. WHAT'S EXPECTED OF ME? is a touching human portrait that conveys both the anxiety and promise of the awkward passage between childhood and adolescence.

Theresa Mack was a Portapak pioneer, using video first in therapeutic situations, then moving on to teach video to children at Young Filmmakers and at Teacher's and Writer's Collaborative in New York City. She has worked with her husband, Dan Mack, producing documentaries for NBC's "The Today Show."

Artists/Producers Index

Palfi, Stevenson J.
This Cat Can Play Anything
Piano Players Rarely Ever
Play Together
Paper Tiger Collective
"Paper Tiger Television"/
Herb Schiller Reads the
New York Times—712
Pages of Waste: *The
Sunday Times*
Parkerson, Michelle
Gotta Make This Journey:
Sweet Honey in the Rock
Phillips, Liz
30 Second Spots
Pomer, Karen
MOVE: Confrontation in
Philadelphia
Powell, Alan
Algebra and Other Menstrual
Confusions
Pratt, Greg
In the Midst of Plenty
A Man Writes to a Part of
Himself: The Poetry of
Robert Bly

Ramos, Tony
30 Second Spots
Ranucci, Karen
Disarmament Video Survey
Raymond, Alan
The Police Tapes
Raymond, Susan
The Police Tapes
Reeves, Dan
Sabda
Smothering Dreams
Reich, Steve
30 Second Spots
Reilly, John
Giving Birth: Four Portraits
The Irish Tapes
The Pursuit of Happiness
Rosenquist, Willard
Video: The New Wave
Rosler, Martha
A Simple Case for Torture,

Or How Not to Sleep at
Night
Rugoff, Ralph
The Best Place to Live

St. Nuñez, Angel
Video: The New Wave
Sanborn, John
Interpolation
Sandin, Dan
Video: The New Wave
Santos, Carlos
30 Second Spots
Seawright, James
Video: The New Wave
Serra, Richard
Video: The New Wave
Shepard, Sam
Tongues
Simon, Fred
Frank: A Vietnam Veteran
Video: The New Wave
Smith, Michael
It Starts at Home
Steina
Selected Treecuts
Video: The New Wave
Stern, Rudi
Video: The New Wave
Sweeney, Skip
My Father Sold Studebakers
Sweetnam, Elizabeth
Shopping Bag Ladies

Teitelbaum, Richard
30 Second Spots
Tejada-Flores, Rick
Low 'N Slow, The Art of
Lowriding
Tolan, Sandy
Disarmament Video Survey
Top Value Television (TVTV)
Four More Years
The Lord of the Universe
Video: The New Wave
Tsuno, Keiko
Chinatown: Immigrants in
America
Cuba: The People

Subject Index

Adolescence

Art

Black Issues

Computer Video

Algebra and Other Menstrual
    Confusions
Artifacts
Barbara Buckner: Selected Work
Deadline
Happenstance
Montana
Selected Treecuts
Sunstone
Travels

Dance

Ballet Classes: A Celebration
The Four Seasons
30 Second Spots
Video: The New Wave

Documentary

Ama L'Uomo Tuo (Always
    Love Your Man)
American Grizzly: Frederick
    Manfred
Ballet Classes: A Celebration
The Best Place to Live
Black, White and Married
Cape May: End of the Season
Changes
Chinatown: Immigrants in
    America
A Common Man's Courage
Cuba: The People
Dairy Queens
Days of Swine and Roses
Disarmament Video Survey
Ends of the Earth: Plaquemines
    Parish, LA
Four More Years
Frank: A Vietnam Veteran
Giving Birth: Four Portraits
Gotta Make This Journey:
    Sweet Honey in the Rock

Grenada: Portrait of a
    Revolution
Hamper McBee: Raw Mash
Healthcare: Your Money or
    Your Life
In the Midst of Plenty
The Irish Tapes
L.A. Nickel
The Lord of the Universe
The Love Tapes, Series 18
Low 'N Slow, The Art of
    Lowriding
A Man Writes to a Part of
    Himself: The Poetry of
    Robert Bly
Mayday Realtime
Media Burn
Meta Mayan II
Monterey's Boat People
MOVE: Confrontation in
    Philadelphia
My Father Sold Studebakers
Oblique Strategist Too
"Paper Tiger Television"/Herb
    Schiller Reads the *New*
    York Times—712 Pages of
    Waste: *The Sunday Times*
Piano Players Rarely Ever Play
    Together
Pick Up Your Feet: The Double
    Dutch Show
The Police Tapes
Presumed Innocent
The Pursuit of Happiness
Running with the Bulls
Shopping Bag Ladies
Signed, Sealed, and Delivered:
    Labor Struggle in the Post
    Office
Smothering Dreams
Some of These Stories Are True
The Stag Hotel
This Cat Can Play Anything
The 21st Annual World
    Eskimo-Indian Olympics
Vietnam: Picking up the Pieces
What's Expected of Me?

Drama

Tongues

Ethnic Issues

The Best Place to Live
Chinatown: Immigrants in
    America
Low 'N Slow, The Art of
    Lowriding
Monterey's Boat People
The 21st Annual World
    Eskimo-Indian Olympics

Families

Giving Birth: Four Portraits
My Father Sold Studebakers
The Pursuit of Happiness
What's Expected of Me?

Health

Healthcare: Your Money or
    Your Life

Humor

Always Late
The Best of William Wegman
Cape May: End of the Season
Days of Swine and Roses
It Starts at Home

Justice

MOVE: Confrontation in
    Philadelphia
The Police Tapes
Presumed Innocent

Labor

Signed, Sealed, and Delivered:
    Labor Struggle in the Post
    Office

Latin America

Cuba: The People
Grenada: Portrait of a
    Revolution
Meta Mayan II

Media Criticism

Dara Birnbaum: Selected Work
Four More Years
It Starts at Home
Media Burn
"Paper Tiger Television"/Herb
    Schiller Reads the *New
    York Times*—712 Pages of
    Waste: *The Sunday Times*
Perfect Leader
A Simple Case for Torture, Or
    How Not to Sleep at Night
Smothering Dreams

Men's Issues

American Grizzly: Frederick
    Manfred
Running with the Bulls
Smothering Dreams
Some of These Stories Are True
The Stag Hotel

Music

Gotta Make This Journey:
    Sweet Honey in the Rock
Hamper McBee: Raw Mash
Oblique Strategist Too

151

153

Distributors List

Adair Films
2051 Third Street
San Francisco, CA 94107
415-621-6500

Alturas Films
2752A Folsom Street
San Francisco, CA 94110
415-285-3984

Ann St. Productions
42 Ann Street
New York, NY 10038

Best Place Video
21 Irving Avenue
Providence, RI 02906
401-351-6923

Black Filmmaker Foundation
WNYC-TV
One Centre Street, 27th floor
New York, NY 10007
212-619-2480

Skip Blumberg
69 Reade Street
New York, NY 10007
212-732-1725

Castelli/Sonnabend
142 Greene Street
New York, NY 10012
212-431-6279

The Center for International
    Education (CIE)
Box 65343
St. Paul, MN 55165
612-227-2240

The Center for New American
    Media
524 Broadway, 2d floor
New York, NY 10012
212-925-5665

Dennis Darmek
2627 North Stowell Avenue
Milwaukee, WI 53211
414-963-9697

Downtown Community
    Television Center (DCTV)
87 Lafayette Street
New York, NY 10013
212-966-4510

Electronic Arts Intermix (EAI)
10 Waverly Place, 2d floor
New York, NY 10003
212-473-6822

Global Village
454 Broome Street
New York, NY 10012
212-966-7526

Philip Mallory Jones
Box 52
Ithaca, NY 14851

The Kitchen
Video Distribution
59 Wooster Street
New York, NY 10012
212-925-3615

Korine-Dunlop
1956 McLendon Avenue N.E.
Atlanta, GA 30307
404-373-3853

Mary Lucier
223 West 20th Street, Apt. 4A
New York, NY 10011
212-255-4947

James Morris
342 Holyoke Street
San Francisco, CA 94134
415-468-2171

Museum of Modern Art
Film/Video Circulating
Department
ll West 53rd Street
New York, NY 10019
212-708-9530

Spencer Nakasako
3101 Ellis Street
Berkeley, CA 94703
415-845-4730

New Front Programming
Services
1409 Willow Street, Suite 505
Minneapolis, MN 55403
612-872-0805

New Orleans Video Access
Center (NOVAC)
2010 Magazine Street
New Orleans, LA 70130
504-524-8626

Paper Tiger Television
165 West 91st Street
New York, NY 10024
212-362-5287

The Pennsylvania State
University
Audio Visual Services
Special Services Building
University Park, PA 16802
814-863-3102

Shadow Projects Inc.
462 Broome Street
New York, NY 10013
212-925-9605

Fred Simon Productions
43 Myrtle Street
Norfolk, MA 02056
617-528-7279

Stevenson Productions Inc.
3227 Banks Street
New Orleans, LA 70119
504-822-7678

TAMERIK Productions
237 Second Street
Jersey City, NJ 07302
201-656-8157

Temple University
Dept. of Radio-Television-Film
Film/Video Distribution Center
Annenberg Hall
Philadelphia, PA 19122
215-787-8483

TVG Documentary Arts
Project, Inc.
Box 315
Franklin Lakes, NJ 07417
201-891-8240

UCVideo
425 Ontario Street S.E.
Minneapolis, MN 55414
612-376-3333

VFC Productions
Box 813
Brookline Village, MA 02147

The Vasulkas
Rte 5, Box 100
Santa Fe, NM 87501
505-983-8128

Video Data Bank
280 South Columbus
Chicago, IL 60603
312-443-3793

Video Free America
442 Shotwell Street
San Francisco, CA 94110
415-648-9040

Video Repertorie
31 Greene Street
New York, NY 10013
212-966-6326

Video Verite
927 Madison Avenue
New York, NY 10021
212-249-7356

Women Make Movies
19 West 21st Street
New York, NY 10010
212-929-6477

Photo Credits

Ballet Classes: A Celebration
Jack Churchill
Photo credit *Margaret
Richardson*
The Best of William Wegman
William Wegman
Photo credit *Michael
Danowski*
Chott el-Djerid (A Portrait in
Light and Heat) *Bill Viola*
Photo credit *Kira Perov*
Dara Birnbaum: Selected Work
Dara Birnbaum
Photo credit *Dara Birnbaum*
Deadline *Max Almy*
Photo credit *Michael
Danowski*
Four More Years *TVTV*
Photo credit *Michael
Danowski*
The Four Seasons *Eva Maier*
Photo credit *Michael
Danowski*
Global Groove *Nam June Paik*
Photo credit *Michael
Danowski*
Gotta Make This Journey:
Sweet Honey in the Rock
Michelle Parkerson
Photo credit *Don Vafiades*
Hamper McBee: Raw Mash
*Blaine Dunlop and Sol
Korine*
Photo credit *Robert Jones*

Hatsu Yume (First Dream) *Bill
Viola*
Photo credit *Kira Perov*
Healthcare: Your Money or
Your Life *Keiko Tsuno and
Jon Alpert*
Photo credit *C. Brownie
Harris*
It Starts at Home *Michael
Smith*
Photo credit *Kevin Noble*
L.A. Nickel *Branda Miller*
Photo credit *Michael
Danowski*
A Man Writes to a Part of
Himself: The Poetry of
Robert Bly *Mike Hazard
and Greg Pratt*
Photo credit *Rick Snider*
Mayday Realtime *David Cort*
Photo credit *Michael
Danowski*
Media Burn *Ant Farm*
Photo credit *Michael
Danowski*
Meta Mayan II *Edin Velez*
Photo credit *Ethel Velez*
Oblique Strategist Too *Edin
Velez*
Photo credit *Ethel Velez*
Ohio to Giverny: Memory of
Light *Mary Lucier*
Photo credit *Kevin Brunelle*
Paper Tiger Television: Herb
Schiller Reads the *New*